OUT OF THE ROUGH

OUT OF THE ROUGH

Booze, Birdies and a Driving Ambition:
the Story of Barclay Howard

**Barclay Howard
with Jonathan Russell**

MAINSTREAM
PUBLISHING

EDINBURGH AND LONDON

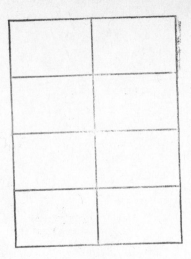

First published in Great Britain in 2001 by
MAINSTREAM PUBLISHING COMPANY (EDINBURGH) LTD
7 Albany Street
Edinburgh EH1 3UG

ISBN 1 84018 511 2

A catalogue record for this book is available from the British Library

Printed and bound in Great Britain by Butler and Tanner Ltd, Frome and London

CONTENTS

FOREWORD   By Sam Torrance MBE   7

ONE   The Longest Fairway   9

TWO   Teeing Off   15

THREE   The Tournament Golfer   23

FOUR   International Golfer – and Drinker   33

FIVE   The Eternal Battle   59

SIX   Burning up the Fairways   75

SEVEN   Open Glory   111

EIGHT   What's Wrong With Me?   135

NINE   'Please Kill Me'   161

TEN   Back on the Tee   185

FOREWORD

By Sam Torrance MBE

The first time I met Barclay Howard there were two things which struck me about him. One was his unmistakable golfing talent and the other was his engaging personality. Even as a teenager, Barclay was good fun to be around on and off the golf course.

Our first encounter on the course was in the West of Scotland Boys Championship final in 1969. I won 3 and 2 but we got on like a house on fire, and from that moment on I've always taken a keen interest in his career in amateur golf.

Barclay was supremely talented, a strong player who I expected to join the professional ranks at some stage. I still think he would have enjoyed a successful career if he had decided to join the rest of us on the European Tour, but he clearly enjoyed combining his work with amateur golf.

When I moved to England to begin my pro career our paths didn't cross that often, but I was frequently aware of his name cropping up in the newspapers as he won numerous amateur titles and achieved his ultimate ambition of representing Great Britain and Ireland in the Walker Cup.

The 1997 Open Championship at Royal Troon was something which captured the imagination of the Scottish public. It's not often that amateur golfers of Barclay's vintage – I have to be careful here! – find themselves right at the top of the leaderboard in a championship of that magnitude.

I have been fortunate enough to experience the thrill of holing the putt which clinched the Ryder Cup in 1985 and I have contended for important titles all over the world, but the reception you receive at the eighteenth green at an Open in Scotland plays havoc with the emotions.

I know Barclay savoured every moment of that sustained applause at Troon as he finished the Championship on Sunday afternoon. It was richly deserved. It can be tough enough to qualify for the Open, never mind complete the 72 holes.

He showed that day that he was a fighter, a real battler who never knew he was beaten until it was time to shake hands. Those qualities, I believe, sustained him when he was diagnosed with leukaemia shortly after the 1997 Walker Cup.

Like everyone else, I was shocked to hear the news, but I knew that if anyone could beat that illness, Barclay could. It is to his eternal credit that he coped with his condition with great fortitude, always resilient and always convinced he would make a full recovery. He was a tenacious competitor in that West of Scotland Boys final all those years ago and that resolve is still there in abundance.

It is wonderful to see him restored to rude health again. No one deserves it more.

ONE

The Longest Fairway

The Jimmy Heggarty Trophy is hardly one of the biggest championships in golf. The Cathkin Braes club where it is played certainly boasts a lovely course, nestling in the fields between Busby and East Kilbride, to the south-east of Glasgow, and it is usually an enjoyable 36-hole event which attracts some good amateur players from around Scotland. As a tournament, however, it is unlikely ever to warrant any media attention other than a few lines in the local paper, or to be graced by the likes of Tiger Woods or Colin Montgomerie. In contrast, I have been the focus of worldwide media attention for playing golf and have had the chance to line up alongside Woods, Montgomerie and many of the other best players in the world. I have even led, albeit briefly, the greatest tournament of them all, the Open, and been involved in nail-biting drama in the Walker Cup. Yet I have never been so nervous as I was teeing the ball up at the first hole at Cathkin Braes on a sunny day in June 2000. I had won the Jimmy Heggarty Trophy a couple of times previously. In fact I had won more than 100 amateur golf tournaments previously. But the shot I was about to hit, my first of that year's tournament, meant more to me than any other in my long playing career. It was also the first shot I had hit in competitive golf for nearly three years.

The summer of 1997 was a glorious time for me. I was playing the best golf of my life and had qualified for the Open, being held that year at the Royal Troon course in Ayrshire. Since I was a small boy pottering around the practice ground at Cochrane Castle Golf Club, in my home town of Johnstone, I had dreamed of playing at the Open. Countless well-meaning people had told me over the years that I was good enough to play with the professionals but I'd just never got round to turning pro. Marriages, work and a strong predilection for alcohol had combined to keep me in the amateur ranks. In July 1997, however, I was there holding my own with the very best players in the world. At one stage on the first day I had a share of the lead, and a fairly straightforward putt would have allowed me to take it outright, but my nerve let me down. Afterwards, it seemed like every newspaper and television company in the world wanted to know about me. In particular they wanted to know how a recovering alcoholic, who used to pack his golf bag with cans of super-strength lager and vodka, was able to compete with the cream of the world's golfers.

Six weeks after hitting the headlines at the Open I was back in the news again, but this time on the front pages instead of the back. This time it was not a success story of how I had battled back from the seemingly bottomless pit of alcoholism to enjoy fleeting fame. Instead it was the tragic story of how I had contracted leukaemia and been told that I might die. During my subsequent battle with the disease there were certainly times when I wished I was dead as I suffered immense pain and sickness. The illness also had a devastating effect on my family. My elderly mother had to face the possibility that she might have to watch her only son die a slow, agonising death. My wife was reduced to tears every time someone innocently asked how my treatment was progressing. Our daughter, only five years old when the cancer was diagnosed, was too young to understand what was going on. All she knew was that her daddy was desperately ill and her mummy was very, very sad.

This was, however, the second time I'd suffered a life-threatening illness, although the first was entirely self-inflicted. It took me years to admit to myself I was an alcoholic. My family and friends realised long before I did and tried to help me, but I wouldn't listen. As far as I was concerned I liked a drink, sometimes a bit too much, but that was all there was to it. I certainly didn't consider myself an alcoholic. My second marriage broke up, my friends gradually left me one by one and I was told that I would never represent my country at golf again, all because of my drinking. But still I would not face up to the fact that I had a serious problem.

Finally, in 1991, I was banned from the game I loved for a year and was faced with a stark choice. I could either be honest with myself and get help, or I could carry on burying my head in the sand, finding my only pleasure in life at the bottom of a bottle of lager so strong it tasted like rocket fuel, and slowly drink myself to death. If I'd chosen the latter option I have little doubt that I wouldn't be here writing these words. You see, it wasn't simply that I liked to drink, I needed to. For several years, my whole life revolved around getting through the working week so that I could fly out of work straight to the nearest off-licence on a Friday. I would then buy the strongest lager and vodka I could lay my hands on and drink until I passed out. Frequently I would have to be up early the next morning to play in a golf tournament, but I soon realised that as I sobered up on the course my game would go to pieces. It seemed the most sensible course of action, therefore, was to ensure that I wouldn't sober up during a crucial round, and so I would booze my way through 18 or even 36 holes. Almost unbelievably I won a host of golf tournaments thanks to, or perhaps despite, this somewhat dubious tactic. Sadly, however, my fondness for booze almost wrecked my whole life. As I told the *Daily Telegraph*'s Robert Philip shortly after the Open: 'From the age of 18 to 38 my life was a mess. If you wanted to do something wrong then all you had to do was come to me. I'm the expert. I wrote the book. I was fast disappearing down a big black hole until I gave up the juice.'

I do believe, however, that if I had not already gone through my struggle with alcohol addiction, I would not have believed I had the courage or strength to beat such a devastating condition as cancer. I did beat it though, and every day of my battle I dreamed of playing golf again.

That is why, as I stood on the first tee at Cathkin Braes that day, I had never been so nervous about hitting a golf ball in my life. So many moments from my life went through my head as I stood there. All through my cancer treatment I had dreamed of playing golf again. At times it seemed like an impossible dream, but I was determined never to give up. Now here I was back doing what I loved more than anything else in the world. It had been a long wait but, whatever was going to happen with that shot and with the rest of the round, it was going to have been worth it. In fact, I doubt if any player in history has gained as much satisfaction from one shot as I did that day.

As I write this I have beaten my cancer and am working ferociously hard to regain the strength I lost through the terrible muscle wastage I suffered as a result of being bedridden for a year. Alcoholism, on the other hand, is an illness for which there is no final cure. What I can say is that I have not had a drink since 1997, and I've not been a hard drinker since 1991. That is something of which I am very proud, but it does not mean I've recovered. It means I'm *recovering*. Like everyone who has ever plumbed the depths I did before facing up to reality, I will always be an alcoholic. Nowadays, however, I'm an alcoholic who doesn't drink. I would be scared to have even one drink these days for fear of what it would lead to. I know that if I never have that first drink then I can never have the 10th, or 12th or 20th. Yes, it can be hard at times and I do still get longings to drink. That's when the love and support of my family and friends is such an inspiration. Without them I would not have conquered these two illnesses. I can't pretend that it has been easy, but hopefully somebody, somewhere, who has a drink problem or is suffering from a serious illness, will read this book and realise that no matter how desperate the situation seems there is still hope.

My name is Barclay and I'm an alcoholic. This is my story.

TWO

Teeing Off

It was inevitable that I would play golf, growing up as I did just 100 yards from the Cochrane Castle course. My father, David, had joined the club in 1954 – the year after I was born – when the membership fee was four guineas and, from as far back as I can remember, I would spend every spare second I had there. My dad, who played off a handicap of 14, worked long hours driving a digger in the local quarry in our hometown of Johnstone; a tough, largely working-class town about 12 miles from Glasgow. The long hours he spent at work made him cherish his weekly Saturday golf game. From about the time I could walk, I would join him on the course, following him round and watching as he would use these long sticks to hit a small white ball around the countryside. I was mystified but desperate to join in. I longed to have my own set of clubs so that I could knock the ball around too. When I did get my own clubs, a left-handed half set which, as a right-handed four-year-old, were not ideal and far too big for me, they were all I was interested in.

From then on I would spend every second I had either playing holes or just knocking a ball around the practice area. In the summertime my dad would leave the quarry at lunchtime and I'd meet him on the third tee. We'd play the third and fourth holes, with him dressed in his boiler suit, before he headed back to work. On Saturday evenings he would take me and my sister Morag, who's six years older than me, to the thirteenth tee, which was the nearest point of the course to our house in Bruce Avenue, and we would all play the last six holes together.

I was enthralled with the game of golf from the first time I hit the ball. My parents never had to push me to practise because I just loved doing it. The fact I was using left-handed clubs in my early days didn't bother me at all, but my dad obviously knew that, as a right-hander, I would find it easier if I changed over. The chance came when I turned seven and was given the junior membership at Cochrane Castle I'd been longing for. In a way it didn't make much difference as I was already spending all my spare time there. I'm sure some of the members must have thought I just pitched a tent somewhere on the course at night. In the club's official centenary book, published in 1995, author William Mitchell wrote about me: 'Blessed with a rare, natural talent, he never required to learn to play golf – it was inborn. Older members can recall the chunky figure in short trousers who, morning, noon and night, haunted the course during school holidays making the game look ridiculously easy.' It's just about spot on, though I'm still hurt by the 'chunky' description!

At that time Cochrane Castle had a clubmaster who was employed basically to look after the day-to-day running of the club and clubhouse. His name was Alex Bain and he knew my dad well. Alex's son had played golf but lost interest, and a deal was struck for my father to buy his right-handed clubs for me. When I set eyes on my new clubs I couldn't believe my luck. I thought all my Christmases had come at once. If my mother didn't see much of me before, she was about to see even less now.

Every spare minute was spent at the golf club. During the school holidays I would disappear out of the door straight after breakfast and not return until it was too dark to see the ball. I loved playing with a group of friends and we would regularly play three rounds a day. My mum would keep watch out of the window for me and, when she spotted me, would bring sandwiches and a drink to the fence at the thirteenth tee to keep me going. There were time restrictions when juniors were not allowed on the course, but this didn't stop me. I would just head for the practice ground and hit endless shots, pretending to be my hero Jack Nicklaus.

I know most people look back fondly on their early childhood days, but I really don't think mine could have been any happier. I even loved primary school, which was also called Cochrane Castle, but I still longed for the bell to ring every day so I could run home, grab my clubs and head for the course. It's safe to say homework was not a particularly high priority of mine. I played right-back for the school football team but, while I enjoyed football, it was very much a second love, although rounds of golf would often be interrupted for an impromptu kickabout in the rough next to the fifteenth green. One of my classmates back then was a certain David Livingstone. Not the great explorer, but the man who now fronts Sky Sports' golf coverage. He was also a member of Cochrane Castle and was one of the pals who would while away the summer holidays with me, playing countless rounds of golf.

At the age of nine, as one of the club's promising youngsters, I was sent with a group of other junior members to receive tuition from Jack Murray, the coach at the Cowglen club in Glasgow. Jack taught me the basics and I would eagerly look forward to my weekly lesson, even if he could be something of an ogre at times. He was very abrupt and we were all scared of him, fearing he could fly off the handle at any moment. But he was a great teacher and he gave me a very solid grounding in all the basics, even if all I wanted to do was copy my idol Jack Nicklaus's swing.

As I approached 12, my dad decided the time had come for me to move up to adult-sized clubs. His job was not particularly well paid and golf clubs are not cheap. So, to make sure he could afford my dream birthday present, he gave up smoking for a year and set aside the money he spent on cigarettes for my birthday fund. I knew what I was getting for my birthday, and when the day came he took me into a sports shop in Glasgow to let me pick out a set. I was wide-eyed when I walked through the door, but as soon as I saw a set bearing the Jack Nicklaus name there was no need to look any further. Those Jack Nicklaus World Series clubs lasted me more than 10 years – and they got a lot of use in every type of weather imaginable.

My father's sacrifice was just one of countless he and my mother made throughout my childhood so they could financially support my interest in golf. It must have been hard for them to afford to keep sending me away to tournaments but they never once grumbled and took pride in watching my game improve. It was the saddest day of my life when my father died in 1976, aged 59. I got a phone call to say he'd had a heart attack and dashed to the hospital to see him on a Saturday morning. The first thing he said to me was: 'Why aren't you at the Ralston Rosebowl tournament?' It was typical of my father to put me and my golf before himself. He died that afternoon and it was a terrible time for me. I really felt the world had lost the greatest man it had ever seen. I was also gutted that, although he had seen me play for Scotland at junior and youth level, he died before I managed to break into the senior team. When I've had success on the golf course, such as the 1995 Walker Cup and the 1997 Open, I have often thought about how much I owe him and how proud he would be of me. Hopefully he has been able to look down and watch from heaven. I'm sure he would like to give me a good hiding for the way I've behaved because of alcohol. But I'm also sure he would think that all the time and money he invested in my golf was more than worth it.

As I got older, golf took on an increasing importance in my life – especially as my love of school disappeared the moment I went to secondary. Most of my friends went to the local high school in Johnstone and I was desperate to go with them. My parents, however, decided I would go to the local posh school, the fee-paying John Neilson Institute in Paisley. I hated it from the moment I walked through the door. In fact I probably hated it even before then – when I put on the wine-red blazer and cap that first morning. I'm sure there was nothing wrong with the school, it just wasn't where I wanted to be. All my pals would be walking to Johnstone High in the morning while I'd be heading for the bus stop, getting teased for my ridiculous uniform. Despite hating every minute of it I still gained six O Grades, but had no desire to stay on any longer than necessary. Anyway, all I wanted to be in life was a professional golfer, and I didn't see how memorising endless mathematical formulae or quoting dull Shakespearean soliloquies was going to help me in that line of work.

So, as I advanced through secondary school, the ratio of time devoted to golf compared to education widened even further. It didn't matter to me what the weather was like, if the course or practice area were playable then I would be there. In fact I preferred it when it was raining as most other people would stay indoors, giving me the run of the practice ground. It meant I could do whatever I wanted without having to worry about anyone else. All the members must have thought I was mad as they watched from inside.

The school holidays were, naturally, my favourite time. If I wasn't playing rounds of golf with my friends, I would spend all day on the practice ground, working on the tips Jack Murray had given me that week. I would take my bag of balls down and spend the morning hitting anything up to 300 drives. I would then head home for lunch before returning in the afternoon to hit a similar number of irons. Then, after tea, I'd be back again to work on my putting. If the modern-style driving range had been invented then I would probably have hit even more, but I used to get pretty fed up collecting all my balls. I would also regularly soak my hands in methylated spirits to harden up the skin and prevent myself getting blisters.

When I was 13 it was time to move on from Jack Murray, and John Irvine, from Kilmacolm, took up the coaching duties. He was a tremendous teacher who had played professionally for a while. He would liven up the lessons with tales from the world of pro golf and I would just listen, awestruck, as he told me stories about Jack Nicklaus, Arnold Palmer and my other heroes who I read about in my growing collection of golf magazines. He seemed to know the magical cure for every golfing problem and, although Jack had given me my grounding in the important basics, it was John who really set me on the road to becoming a good golfer. And there was nothing else I wanted to be. Several times a season I would head to the golf club on a Saturday night to watch *Shell's Wonderful World of Golf* being shown on the movie projector. I loved watching Nicklaus, Palmer and the other great names of the day and it would feed my ambition to become a professional golfer. If I was to succeed, however, I would have to start playing in tournaments. Up to now I had played a few junior medals at Cochrane Castle but that was it. I pestered my parents to let me try my luck in a serious competition, and in 1966 they decided I was ready. So as a nervous but excited 13-year-old, I headed to the Scottish Boys Championship at North Berwick for my first taste of tournament golf.

THREE

The Tournament Golfer

It wasn't just the thought of playing in my first golf tournament that I was excited about as I headed for North Berwick: it was also my first time away from home without adult supervision. I had been on Boys Brigade camps, but always with the leaders keeping a keen eye on me. This, however, was different. I travelled through with two other Cochrane Castle members – Michael Craig, who was also 13, and Bobby Blackwood, who, as the eldest at 17, was put in charge of our little outing. We stayed at a guest house run by a lady called Mrs Ferguson, who looked upon us as three sons. I was incredibly excited and, as we reached the course on the first day, was desperate to know who my opponent would be. I was drawn against an older lad called John Thompson, who played out of the Kirkhill club in Cambuslang, on the outskirts of Glasgow. When he joined me on the first tee I could hardly believe my eyes. He was about 6 ft 4 in. tall and weighed about 19 stone – at least that's what it looked like to this somewhat overawed 13-year-old. Needless to say, he beat me fairly convincingly, but I didn't care. All that mattered to me was that I'd had my first taste of tournament golf and I was hungry for more.

I had spent the days approaching the tournament feeling tremendously nervous and hardly slept in the nights running up to it. I was worried that if I got too anxious I might make a fool of myself. I decided to confide in my father about my worries. He thought for a while then said he would speak to a pharmacist friend he knew from the golf club. This man, a Mr Robertson, told me there was nothing to worry about. He said he would give me a couple of pills which would ease my anxiety and calm me down. He said if I took one the night before the tournament and another about an hour before teeing off, he could guarantee that my nerves would disappear. I was so desperate to ensure that nothing would ruin my enjoyment of my first golf tournament that I didn't even question this. I followed his instructions and took my tablets. Sure enough, as I stood on the first tee with John Thompson, I was excited, but my knees weren't knocking and my hands weren't shaking so badly that I couldn't hold my driver, which was what I had feared was going to happen. When I returned home to Johnstone at the end of the weekend, my dad asked if the tablets had worked. When I replied that yes, they had really calmed me down and babbled on about how I wouldn't have been able to play without them, a wry smile started to spread across his face. When I asked what was so funny, he confessed that I had been the victim of a giant con. The tablets Mr Robertson had given me had contained nothing but water. He had assured my dad that as long as I believed they were some sort of magical cure for nerves then they would, in all probability, work. It was an early lesson for me in the mysterious workings of the human mind. If only it was that easy to cure a hook or a slice!

As I said, my first foray into the world of tournament golf had left me eager for more and I started to play at every event I could get into. Every spare minute I had would find me on the practice range hitting ball after ball, trying to perfect the basic technique taught to me by Jack Murray and then honed by John Irvine. My scores were getting better and better and I knew it was only a matter of time until I won my first tournament. It happened the following year, 1967, when, as a 14-year-old, I won the 36 Club Memorial Trophy held at the Haggs Castle course in Glasgow. It was a two-round tournament and I was elated to finish two shots clear of the field. I must have been the proudest boy in Scotland as I went up to collect my 'winnings' at the prize-giving – a small silver trophy and a John Letters Silver Goose putter. It was a truly special feeling walking into the house that night, clutching my trophy and new putter, to tell my parents I had won my first tournament. Again, my appetite was whetted for more. Instead of just sitting back and suddenly thinking I was a wonderful golfer, my win just made me hungrier for more success. I don't know if it was possible for me to cram any more practice time in, but I certainly tried.

Among the pals I would practise with at this time was a boy called Ian McCosh, who was a couple of years older than me. He was a very good player and it helped my game a lot to play with and watch someone of his standard. Ian's help was to be invaluable again some 30 years later when he caddied for me at the Open at Royal Troon.

As I was always a very polite boy, most of the members at Cochrane Castle were very good to me. My father had been a member for a number of years and so a lot of them had known me since I was a toddler, trotting round behind him, trying to keep up as he enjoyed his Saturday afternoon round. They would then see me and my sister with him that evening playing the last six holes. In fact, with the amount of time I ended up spending at the club, most of them thought I was more of a permanent fixture than the first tee. It meant that they were happy to pass on help and tips to me, and also give me a bit more leeway over use of the course than a young teenager would normally have been entitled to at that time. When I turned 16, the club agreed to let me upgrade my membership from junior to senior two years early. The junior membership meant I was restricted to playing on the course only at certain times, so I hungrily snapped up the offer, despite the increase in fees. I also got my handicap down to scratch when I was 16, and was still dreaming of life as a professional golfer. It was also the time I moved on again in coaching terms.

I was first selected for the Scottish boys team in 1969, largely thanks to reaching the semi-final of the Scottish Boys Championship at North Berwick where I lost to Robin Fyfe, who went on to win the final at the nineteenth hole. It was a huge honour to represent my country for the first time, even though we lost to England at Dunbar, and I remember how proud my parents were of me. The following year we played the English at Southport and lost again, but I knew that international golf was for me, and I was to get plenty of opportunities for revenge in the years to come.

Scotland recognition meant free coaching and the squad were regularly dispatched down to Newcastle for tuition from the legendary John Jacobs; one of the most famous coaches in the game at that time and author of numerous golf teaching books. All the Scottish boys team members would travel down together on a bus and as I joined them for the first time I was honoured and excited that I was to be taught by such a famous coach. Unfortunately, it quickly became apparent that John and I just didn't hit it off. He tried to totally change my swing and I wasn't having any of it. I had a very upright type of swing with very little shoulder turn. I was really trying to copy the swing of Jack Nicklaus, as he was my hero, but John didn't like it. He tried to get me to flatten my swing out, but I just didn't feel comfortable with that, partly because it didn't suit my somewhat squat build. On one occasion I returned to Scotland after a session with John, trying to remember the tips he had given me. As I tried to swing the way he'd taught me, however, I found I was shanking everything. The next time we went back I explained what was happening and he said: 'Right, let's have a look then.' It took him about 10 seconds to work out what was wrong and correct it, but I complained to him that he should not have tampered with my basic swing in the first place. I don't think he was very impressed with my attitude. As I said, we never really saw eye to eye. John was a great golf coach, but he just wasn't for me I'm afraid.

That year, 1969, was also when I first got to know Sam Torrance properly. He really was a class apart, and all the boys playing tournaments at that time knew who Sam was. He had been marked out at an early age as the best of his bunch and a dead cert to turn professional. His father, Bob, was one of the best golf teachers in the country and he had given Sam a great technique. Sam was also prepared to work extremely hard at his game, and the young players at that time had to measure themselves against him if they wanted to see how good they were.

The only time we played head-to-head was in the final of the West of Scotland Boys Championship in 1969 at Glasgow's Cathcart Castle Golf Club. I played well, but well was never enough to beat Sam and he won the match – and the tournament – 3 and 2. (He was three holes ahead with two left to play.) I always felt that Sam was a bit ahead of me in terms of golfing ability, but that if I played my very best I could be up there competing with him. He was a long hitter with a very good, all-round solid game. He would take a lot of chances on the course but, because he was so good, they would usually pay off. He turned professional just a few weeks later and, with hindsight, I should have done the same. In fact, after that final at Cathcart Castle, his father told me Sam's plans and urged me to do the same. He reckoned I was good enough and considering he was, and still is, one of the most knowledgeable men in the game, I really should have listened to him. By that time, however, I was starting to enjoy wine, women and song a bit too much and was neglecting my game – something that had seemed unthinkable over the previous few years.

It has been fantastic to see Sam do so well over the last 30 years because, apart from his tremendous ability and great attitude to the game, he is also one of the nicest guys in the sport and a real character. I felt for him a few years ago when he was going through tough times with his putting, but since he got a broom-handled putter he has never looked back. He is always tremendously friendly with a ready smile. Like his dad, he has always had a reputation for enjoying a good time and it is a reputation he well and truly earned! He just seemed to inherit his love of golf and partying from his dad. When I was more than fond of a drink in the 1980s, a few people said to me on different occasions: 'Why don't you go and get a lesson from Bob?' I just told them that it would be a waste of time. Not because of his coaching – he's one of the best there is – but because I knew exactly what would happen. We would spend about half an hour on the golf lesson then head into the bar for the rest of the day!

The great thing about having a father who also loved golf was that he was full of encouragement for me. He knew I hated school but loved the game, so he gave me all the backing I could possibly want. Plenty of people in the game told him I would be good enough to turn professional and that's what I kept aiming for. Sadly, it wasn't to happen, if I'm honest, because I stopped devoting as much time to golf, then got a job and married young. I sometimes look at what Sam has achieved and think: 'That could have been me.' But then I think that if I had turned pro I might have got nowhere, become disillusioned with the game and given up, and then I would never have experienced the fantastic times I enjoyed later on as an amateur. I believe in making your choices as you go through life and then living with them. There is no point in regretting things from your past. What's done is done and can't be changed. You just have to get on with life. That's why, although it is sometimes nice to dream about how I could have won a dozen majors if I'd turned professional back then, I'm just grateful for all the good times the game of golf has given me.

BOBBY BLACKWOOD

Boyhood friend

Every member of Cochrane Castle Golf Club in the late 1950s and early 1960s was familiar with the sight of a short, overweight, but very strong figure with a permanent smile fixed to his face, making his way round the course. This was because Barclay Howard was never away from the place. Before we became members we would have to sneak on to the course, but no one seemed to mind, mainly because everyone had known Barclay almost since he could walk. I was a few years older than

Barclay, but we became close pals because we lived just a few yards apart and shared a love of golf. On days when we couldn't get on the course, we would transform Barclay's front garden into a mini driving range and hit irons over his fence onto the course. We would be quite happy hitting hundreds of balls a day like this, because all we wanted to do in life was grow up to be the next Jack Nicklaus.

If we were keen golfers before getting membership, we were practically addicted afterwards. All through the holidays we would spend the entire day playing as many holes of golf as we could, sustained by Mrs Howard's sandwiches and juice delivered to us on the thirteenth tee. Even back then, Barclay lived for the game and would spend every spare moment he had playing or practising. He worked harder at his game than any of the rest of us, and it was also obvious he had a special talent. He also had a talent for getting on the right side of just about everyone he met. As a boy Barclay had a really loveable sort of face. He was quite chubby because he liked his grub so much and he was always smiling so people just took to him. It stood us in good stead when we went on trips to tournaments like the Scottish Boys Championship at North Berwick. The year I went with Barclay and Michael Craig, the landlady at our boarding house took one look at Barclay and practically adopted all three of us on the spot. She treated us like long-lost sons and would send us out each day stuffed full with the biggest breakfasts I'd ever seen. They were no problem for Barclay, however, and anything Michael or I couldn't finish soon disappeared down his throat. The same thing happened after the junior team matches. There were never any sandwiches or cakes left over if Barclay was there – he just devoured the lot. But he always looked incredibly healthy. He was quite plump, as I've said, but it seemed to suit him, and his skin was always so healthy it seemed to glow. He was also very powerful and had strong arms. This helped make him into a tremendous driver off the tee. Even as a child he could smash the ball miles, but as soon as he got up round the greens he was also able to produce some deft shots. He really had a lovely soft touch as well. It was hard to believe someone with so much power could also be so good around the green.

I have never understood why he didn't turn professional. He was certainly good enough, but he just left school and got a job straight away. He married young and the years just seemed to go by. Then, at the time he should have been at the peak of his game, he was getting into a real state with the drink. He would become a different person when he was drunk, and change from this gentle, kind man into someone quite horrible who you would do your best to avoid. It didn't help that a lot of the amateur golf tournaments in those days were sponsored by whisky companies, and after the serious business was over there would be loads of free booze going around. As Barclay was a bit of a star there was always plenty for him, but it just encouraged him to get really drunk, which would inevitably lead to some unpleasant scenes. It was a pity because, after he got his one year ban from golf and stopped drinking, he worked really hard at his game. The Open at Troon gave the world a glimpse of just what he could have achieved if he had kept on the straight and narrow in his younger days.

I watched on the television at home and couldn't believe how well he was playing. But after everything he had been through he deserved all the glory and I was delighted for him. I was stunned when I heard he had fallen ill just a few weeks later, though. After the way he had tackled his earlier problems he did not deserve to suffer something as dreadful as cancer. It was upsetting for me to think of the boy I remembered so well, always so cheery and full of life, lying at death's door. I still see him sometimes up at Cochrane Castle and occasionally think back to those childhood days spent golfing together from dawn to dusk. We both love the game, but what sets Barclay apart from everyone else is that he was put on this earth for one reason – to play golf.

FOUR

International Golfer – and Drinker

As I progressed from boys golf into youth, I am sure my parents were disappointed that I never tried to turn professional. I was playing very well around the ages of 17, 18 and 19, and I believe my father, in particular, wanted me to have a go on the European Tour. He kept saying that I had such a natural talent it was a shame not to see how far it could take me. He really believed I could have done well as a pro. While growing up I had always wanted to turn professional and there is no real explanation for my failure to do so, other than that I never really got round to it. At the crucial time in my late teens where you have to make those sort of decisions, I was more interested in hanging about with my mates, going to pubs and chasing girls than worrying about my future, so it just never happened. Staying in the amateur game did not, however, prevent me from having plenty of goals. After making my last appearance for the Scottish boys team in 1970, I set my sights on getting into the youth team the following year before then moving on to the senior side. Dreams of representing Great Britain and playing in the Walker Cup were also in my mind, but seemed a long way off at that stage.

At first, moving up a level from the comfort zone of being one of the best junior players in the country wasn't easy, and I took a bit of time to settle. Winning my first 36-hole senior tournament in September 1971 – The McLeod Cup at Old Ranfurly Golf Club in Bridge of Weir – proved to me, though, that I could hack it at that level. It was an important milestone for me, but I only got there after a bit of a sweat. After the two rounds I was tied for first place with Murray Rae, from Irvine. This meant the pair of us had to come back the next day for an 18-hole play-off. While I went to bed that night, nervous about what would happen the following morning, I was also excited that I had been able to play good golf while mixing it with the big boys. I was also playing well on a course I liked a lot and knew I had a good chance of winning. The next day I shot a solid 69 to sneak victory by one shot and pick up my first winner's prize in senior golf – a gold bracelet valued at £150. Not a bad prize for an 18-year-old in 1971.

At that time I was spending virtually every weekend driving to tournaments all over Scotland in my father's car. I had no interest in the 18-hole events, I wanted to prove myself in 36- and 72-hole competitions, as those were the ones that the international selectors looked at. But, although I was improving and getting some good results, I wasn't as interested in practising as I should have been, and wasn't showing the dedication needed to get the best out of myself. It was only in the 1990s, after I had dried out and was working harder on my game than I'd ever done in my life, that I started to look back and wonder what might have been. I have no doubt that if I had shown the same level of commitment in the 1970s as I was to do 20 years later, then anything could have been possible. I'm sure there are probably countless sportsmen everywhere who could say the same. It really is true that youth is wasted on the young.

The only downside to my life in 1971 was starting work at the Clydesdale Bank. Without intending to show disrespect to the bank or anyone who works there, it was a nightmare. The money was awful and, as a trainee, I was obviously at the bottom of the pile. The only saving grace was that they used to send me all over the country to play golf for them. I would be packed off to great courses like Gleneagles and St Andrews to represent the Clydesdale in matches against other banks. That, as far as I could see, was the only plus point about working there.

Still, I was happy. I was playing golf at weekends and messing about with my pals at night. One of the highlights of that year for me was reaching the semi-finals of the Scottish Amateur Championship, despite being beaten 5 and 4 by the legendary Charlie Green on the Old Course at St Andrews. I say legendary because he is one of the most famous names in Scottish amateur golf. He was a wonderful player who made several Walker Cup teams. He had a fantastic appetite for the game and I learned a lot just from that one round with him. Being slightly in awe of him, I didn't allow myself to go out and play my natural game. I three putted a lot that day because I was being more aggressive than usual. I kept thinking I had to hole every one because I was up against such a legend. Despite taking quite a heavy beating that day it was a valuable experience for me. Against all the odds, Charlie lost the final the next day to Sandy Stephen who, at 18, became the youngest player to win the title. Performances like reaching the semi-finals of the Scottish Amateur helped to ensure I achieved my goal of being picked for the Scottish youth team for the first time that year and, as a bonus, also made the Great Britain and Ireland youth side to play against the rest of Europe.

By 1972 I was well established in the Scottish senior game and won the West of Scotland stroke average – the best 10 aggregate scores from tournaments in the area – for the first of nine times. I was helped by a record round at the Cathcart Castle course in Glasgow. My victory that day in the Parlane McFarlane Trophy was memorable for an eagle at the fifteenth where I holed a three wood, followed by three birdies at the last three holes for a 63.

In 1972 I also married my first wife, Sandra. I was only 19 and was far too young to get married, but at that age you think you know everything and can do anything. Sandra also worked at the Clydesdale Bank. We had two daughters – Linda, who was born in 1972, and Lorraine who came along four years later. I left the bank in 1973 when a member of Cochrane Castle fixed me up with a job at the Rolls Royce factory at Hillington, on the outskirts of Glasgow. It meant I was bringing in more money but, sadly, not enough to support a family on. So, four nights a week I would drive an ice-cream van to earn extra cash. It meant leaving for work at Rolls Royce at quarter to eight in the morning and not returning, until after my ice-cream shift, at 11 o'clock at night. I was permanently exhausted and hardly had any time to practise my golf. It also meant that Sandra hardly saw me, because as soon as the weekend came round I'd be off to play in a tournament somewhere. Then, when we were together, we just argued and eventually decided that enough was enough. We got married soon after Sandra fell pregnant with the first of our two children. My parents weren't thrilled at first as they wanted me to give it a go as a professional golfer and knew marriage and fatherhood would probably prevent that. But they came round to the idea and were pleased for me, although they had the usual worries about marrying and having children too young. The main source of disharmony in the marriage was money. I was holding down two jobs to make ends meet but Sandra just kept spending everything I earned. Every week she would buy something new for the house, like a sofa or fridge and we just couldn't afford it. The final straw came when we were threatened with eviction because she had not paid the rent for six months. I used to hand over all my wages to Sandra and she would take care of our finances. But, while she was buying all these lovely things for the house, she wasn't bothering to pay the bills and my entire month's wages had to go on clearing the rent arrears. We were left with about two pounds to survive on for the whole month. Eventually I'd had enough and went home to my mum's for a month. I then moved back in with Sandra and the girls but it just wasn't working. It was just a typical story of two people getting married too young and it wasn't surprising that we split up six years after marrying. Looking back, I suppose it is a miracle the marriage lasted that long, and I can see Sandra's point of view that there was no point in having a husband who was hardly ever there. But I had to do the ice-cream run because we badly needed the cash, and there was no way I could have given up the golf. I loved playing in the weekend tournaments and the sport was the driving force behind my whole life.

My big regret is later losing touch with our daughters, Linda and Lorraine. After the marriage ended I stayed in touch for a few years and would see the girls every couple of weeks. It reached the stage, however, where there were fights every time I saw them and they seemed reluctant to see me any more. Eventually, contact just stopped and it has been years since I heard from them, which is sad. I supported the girls financially right up until they were 18 but Sandra was always going on about how I should give them more. The girls would take her side and the whole scene was very unpleasant. It basically just became better for everyone when we stopped seeing each other. Obviously I regret that I wasn't around to watch them grow up properly and that I now know next to nothing about them, although I occasionally hear on the grapevine what they are up to and they both seem to be doing well. I have thought of contacting them but I really believe it would cause a lot of aggravation.

Despite my personal problems, and although I had little time to practise, I was still playing well in the weekend tournaments and winning more than my fair share. I had been encouraged by my taste of international youth golf in 1972, and I made the Scotland, along with the Great Britain and Ireland teams the following three years. In fact, I captained both sides in 1974. Sam Torrance, my team-mate in the Scotland boys teams, had turned professional by this time and, not surprisingly, turned out to be the pick of the bunch from those years. One of my youth team-mates was also to become a Ryder Cup player and captain. Englishman Mark James and I played together for Great Britain and Ireland and it was obvious from the start that he was going to be a very good player. He didn't have a great deal of flair, like a Ballesteros, but he was a very, very solid player who worked hard at his game and deserved the success he went on to achieve. Another player who caught my eye around this time was a 15-year-old called Sandy Lyle. I played two rounds with him in the British Youths Championship at Downfield, in Dundee, in 1974. Ian McCosh was caddying for me and when we saw this young lad's rather wild practice swing on the first tee, we looked at each other as if to say: 'Who does he think he is?' Then he hit the shot and Ian and I looked at each other again in disbelief. He absolutely smashed the ball straight up the middle of the fairway. As we went round it became increasingly obvious that this 15-year-old was going to become a very special player.

He was a fantastic striker of the ball, one of the best I've ever seen, and it was no surprise when he started winning majors.

Also in the team at that time was another Scottish player, David Robertson. He was an exceptional talent and, as a teenager, was generally considered to be the best boy golfer in the world. He could hit every shot in the book and was believed by everyone in the game to be a star in the making. He is probably the only player every to represent his country in boys, youth and senior internationals in the same year. He is certainly the youngest, being only 14 at the time. He was not, however, popular with the other players as he could be very arrogant, and for quite some time there were mutterings that he was cheating. Nobody doubted he had a superb gift for golf, but there was a definite cloud hanging over his honesty on the green. Nothing was proven until the qualifying rounds for the Open in 1985. David was caught replacing his ball in the wrong part of the green – closer to the hole. He was banned for 20 years by the PGA (Professional Golfers Association), although the sentence was lifted seven years later. It was a tragedy as he was an unbelievable player who could have had the world at his feet. Instead, he will always be remembered as somebody who cheated, which is a real shame. Back in the mid-1990s, after his ban had been lifted, he was playing well in tournaments again and there was talk of him getting back into the Scotland side. That caused a bit of a stir as a number of the players who knew him in his youth simply didn't want to play in the same side as him. Some players would probably have refused to play for their country if David had been included. But with my past I can hardly argue that people should not be given a second chance. In 1996 a reporter asked me if David should be allowed back into the Scotland side if he was playing well enough. I replied: 'The past is the past. If he plays well enough to get picked for

Scotland, you've got to give the guy a chance.' And I meant it. But if I had been asked to play with him in the foursomes then I wouldn't have hesitated to say: 'No chance.'

By the late 1970s I felt I was on the verge of a call up to the full Scotland team. I packed in the ice-cream van job when my marriage to Sandra broke up in 1978, which gave me more time to practise. The improvement was immediate as I won ten tournaments that year, and at one stage held half a dozen course records. These included the Sandyhills course where my 62 in winning the Deans Trophy included a back nine where I took just 27 shots. Incredibly, these included a penalty shot! I felt unlucky not to get a senior Scotland call up that year, but my disappointment was forgotten when I finally made the team 12 months later. A second place finish at the Scottish Strokeplay at Rosemount put the seal on my selection for the Home Internationals.

I was beaten at Rosemount by a man who was to become a great friend, and with whom I was to forge a highly successful foursomes partnership for Scotland, Ian Hutcheon. In fact we were unbeaten together in Scotland colours. He beat me by one shot that weekend, but I was still pleased as, for a while, Hutch was undoubtedly the best amateur golfer in the world. He was a few years older than me, but was so laid back that he was a wonderful partner for a younger, less experienced and slightly nervous international newcomer like myself. I learned a lot about golf just from playing with and watching Hutch. If you couldn't get into a rhythm playing with him then you would never be able to. He was a pleasure to play with.

The Home Internationals in 1979 were due to be played in Ireland that year, but one of the many terrorist outrages which were tearing that country apart at the time took place shortly before we were due to leave. As a result the Scottish and English

Golf Unions refused to allow their teams to travel there. I was gutted. I had spent so many years dreaming of playing for my country at that level, and now it was being snatched from me. The blow was softened when it was announced we would play the English team in a friendly international at Royal Troon instead. I was immensely proud to be part of a team which beat the Auld Enemy that weekend, and was delighted with my contribution of three points from four matches. It had given me a taste for senior international golf and I was thirsting for more. By this time, unfortunately, I was also developing an increasing thirst for something else.

I had always liked going out for a drink, but with all my commitments – golf, holding down two jobs and having a family for most of the 1970s – I didn't really have time to go on the sort of binges that were soon to become a major part of my life. By 1980 I was starting to spend more and more time in the pub or propping up the bars in various golf clubhouses. Looking back, I believe the fine line between enjoying a few pints with friends and becoming an alcoholic was crossed at the 1980 Home Internationals. The event was being held at the wonderful Highland course of Dornoch and I was desperate to give it my best shot after the disappointment of the previous year's tournament being cancelled. A team-mate, Alan Brodie, and I had travelled up a day ahead of the rest of the players and decided to settle down in the bar of the hotel for the night. But I didn't just stay for the night, I was there well into the next morning. Alan retired defeated at about 2 a.m., but I was still going strong at 5 a.m. Luckily, we only had to practise the next day, but I was still sticking to this 'routine' when the action got under way. Amazingly, I didn't play too badly but I was certainly far from 100 per cent. Then again, how could anyone do themselves justice with the sort of preparation I was having?

Each night I would drink until the early hours of the morning, grab little more than a couple of hours sleep, then expect to beat the best amateur golfers in Britain. I was kidding myself. Each day I would be playing someone who'd had an early night, while I would have got myself ready the night before by knocking back a dozen pints. It was pathetic, and it is a miracle I contributed any points to the team at all. I certainly didn't deserve to. This set the tone for my international appearances for the next four years. I would love representing my country at golf, but I would love getting tanked up even more. The problem was that by this stage I found it impossible just to have a few quiet drinks. I would have to drink myself into oblivion every time. If I had just one pint then that would be it; I would have to have a major session.

In 1980 I was also selected for the Great Britain and Ireland team for the first time, to play against the Rest of Europe in the St Andrews Trophy at Royal St George's. I did not play in the afternoon singles on the second day but was expected, quite rightly, to be out and about on the course, cheering on the rest of the lads. Before heading out, however, I decided to have a quick pint in the bar and watch a bit of the tennis action from Wimbledon that was on the television at the time. I then spent three hours throwing lager down my throat and managed to catch just the last few holes of the golf action. It was an indefensible and selfish thing to do, but alcohol was fast becoming the most important thing in my life. Even more important than golf.

Somehow, despite the fact that I would spend almost every Friday, Saturday and Sunday night paralytic, I was still playing well enough in the early 1980s to make the Scotland team. Thanks to my increasing fondness for the booze however, my international career was about to come to a grinding halt.

On the way back from the 1983 Home Internationals in Dublin I got completely and utterly wrecked. By this stage I was drinking myself into oblivion almost every weekend but, even by my standards, this was a major, major session. We got the ferry over to Ireland from Holyhead and this was obviously going to mean trouble on the way home. (Fortunately, perhaps, the weather was dreadful on the way over and everyone was too ill to consider having a drink – even me.) I bought an enormous carry-out for the ferry ride, and subsequent bus journey, and started to consume it as quickly as possible. I was extremely drunk for the whole journey, and subjected everyone in the party to the most foul-mouthed abuse imaginable. Nobody was spared. Not team-mates, not the officials, not even the wives who had come to support us. I would just say whatever came into my head, whether I meant it or not. If people spoke to me they got abuse and if they ignored me they got the same. There was no hiding place from the vitriol I was dishing out. I would tell other players why they were useless at golf, the Scottish Golf Union officials why they were freeloaders who knew nothing about the game, and even the poor bus driver probably got a few choice words about his gear changes. I was coming out with absolute rubbish. The next day I could remember nothing, which was becoming an increasingly common occurrence. When I began to hear tales of how I'd behaved, however, I was mortified. I couldn't believe that I could have acted that way, but of course I knew I had, because these morning-after nightmares were becoming increasingly frequent. That was by no means the first time I behaved like a complete idiot while drunk and representing my country, but it was the worst. It was a miracle they didn't ban me from playing for Scotland ever again. I knew I was lucky to get away with it and swore that would be the last time I would drink like that while on international duty. My promise lasted until the very next international.

In June 1984 we played a friendly match against Italy at the Rosemount course in Blairgowrie. I played really well and won all four of my matches, inevitably deciding that this entitled me to a celebratory drinking session at the official post-match meal and function on the last night. I got completely drunk, even though the Scottish Strokeplay Championship was due to start the next day. I was my usual inebriated self, spitting bile and venom at anyone foolish enough to come near me. One of my 'victims' that night was a man I had been friends with for many years, the president of the Scottish Golf Union, David Smith. The next day, when I realised I had been up to my old tricks again, I was mortified. I was to feel worse still when I was told that I'd played my last match for Scotland. An official from the SGU said there would not be any sort of official hearing or ban, but I would simply not be considered for selection anymore. I was devastated, but knew I deserved it. David was a great guy and a good friend who did a lot for Scottish golf. He certainly didn't deserve to be on the receiving end of a mouthful of abuse from me. Once again, I couldn't believe I had been so stupid and was determined not to get in that state again. I vowed I would only have a couple of pints if I was playing golf, but by this time I was an alcoholic and it was impossible for me just to have the odd drink. The problem was that, although I was losing friends fast and people were telling me I had a problem, I just wouldn't admit it. Being told that my Scotland days were over should have been my wake-up call. That should have been the moment I realised the direction in which my life was heading, and I should have sought help there and then. As far as I was concerned though, I just liked a drink, albeit a large one. I didn't have a major problem and I certainly wasn't an alcoholic. Oh no, I could control my drinking, I thought. Only I couldn't.

Instead of realising I urgently had to get control over my drinking, it got worse. Although my international days were over, I was still spending virtually every weekend of the golf season playing in tournaments. I was still doing well, winning a few and was one of the best amateurs in Britain. Unfortunately I was now also one of the best drinkers in Britain. From Monday to Thursday I would usually not touch a drop of alcohol, but when Friday came round it was bedlam. I couldn't wait to get out of work so I could head to the pub, although this became increasingly difficult as the years went by and I was banned from the bars in my home-town one by one. Eventually there wasn't a pub in Johnstone which would serve me. I was barred from every one for subjecting staff and customers to horrendous verbal abuse. It didn't matter if I didn't know the person I was attacking. I would latch on to something about them, and my attacks were poisonous. I'm not remotely religious, but if someone was a Celtic fan I would harangue them for being a Catholic. If someone was fat or bald or short or even if they preferred tea to coffee – it didn't really matter what it was – they would be on the receiving end of the most foul-mouthed rants imaginable. Why I didn't get a good hiding on several occasions I'll never know. I certainly deserved a few.

Getting home from the pub was also a problem as I would always end the night completely paralytic. Fortunately, I had a golden retriever at this time called Jason who was an absolute life-saver. Jason was the quietest and best-natured dog in the world. I used to take him to the pub with me, then he would take me home at the end of the night. Wherever I had been drinking, he would always know how to get home, and I would just clutch on to his lead and allow myself to be dragged along.

He would pull me through hedges and gardens and across roads, and somehow we'd end up at home. He was the best friend I've ever had and I was heartbroken when he died aged only six and a half. Unfortunately, three years earlier, a metal pole had flown off the back of a lorry and hit him on the leg while my mother was walking him. The vet patched him up as best he could, but said Jason would be in pain for the rest of his life. I had to give him painkillers every day which made his life bearable, but eventually they just ruined his liver and kidneys and he had to be put down. It was one of the saddest days of my life as I loved him dearly. There's no doubt that without him I would have spent a lot of nights just sleeping in a ditch or passed out in the street.

His death gave me real problems getting home after many drinking sessions. I would frequently leave the pub and just get on a train to some random destination. The next day I would come round and find myself in another town – often Largs or Stranraer because they were further down the train line that runs from Glasgow to Johnstone. These blackouts were starting to terrify me. I would remember going into a pub and the next thing I knew I would be walking down a street in the middle of another town altogether. Incredibly, I still managed to convince myself that I didn't have a drink problem.

When none of the pubs in Johnstone would serve me any more it just helped my boozing to escalate as it meant I drank at home, which is the worst thing an alcoholic can do. As soon as I got out of work on a Friday I would head straight for the off-licence and pick up some cans of super-strength lager and a bottle of the strongest vodka I could get my hands on. They would taste absolutely foul and the first can was always difficult to get down, but after that I was away and I would drink the whole lot with no problem. Sometimes, if I finished my carry-out early enough, I would head back out to the off-licence and buy the same again. It was a truly appalling way to live, but by this stage all I cared about was drinking. I just loved the buzz I was getting from it and the feeling of not having a care in the world. It didn't occur to me that I was killing myself and losing all my friends in the process.

Drink was the only thing that mattered to me. It was even more important than golf. It was also causing me problems with my game because, as I dried out on a Saturday morning while playing in a tournament after a heavy session the night before, I would start to get the shakes, particularly while putting. So I came up with what I thought at the time was a foolproof plan to solve this. I simply packed my golf bag with booze and drank it on the way round. I would usually put a few cans of lager into my bag, but it wasn't unknown for me to take a half bottle of vodka. The alcohol helped to settle me down while I was playing. If I was drinking lager I would have at least four cans in a round, often more. I used to open the can on the tee, take a swig, lay it down beside my bag, hit my shot and pick it up as I headed up the fairway. I would have finished the can by the start of the next hole and stick it in one of the bins on the tee. When I felt the effects wearing off I would just crack open another one. If I was drinking vodka, I would buy a big bottle of Coke and pour half of it down the sink. I would then fill it up with vodka and just quietly swig away at it on the way round. I used to hear people muttering about how much I liked drinking my Coke during a round. They obviously had no idea about the strong vodka I was taking with it. There were never any officials on the course during the tournaments and none of the other players ever complained, so I just kept on doing it.

All this boozing on the course meant that when I got to the bar at the end of the round with my playing partner to have an after-golf pint, I would already be drunk. Goodness only knows what some people must have thought as I started to talk rubbish after just a few sips. It probably sounds funny to people who conjure up an image in their mind's eye of a golfer getting paralytic on his way round the course and then winning the tournament. I suppose it would be funny if it wasn't so pathetic. But I'm deeply ashamed now when I think back to those times. I mean, what sort of person gets into such a state that he can barely hold his putter steady without taking a swig from a can of lager first?

As I would tend to be drunk by the time I got off the course, I would usually then cause a scene in the clubhouse bar later on by letting someone know exactly what I thought of them. I couldn't count how many winner's speeches I made after golf tournaments while blind drunk. It's a miracle I could even get the words out.

It was hardly surprising that friends began to desert me. If a group of us arranged to meet up in the pub on a Friday or Saturday night I would find myself unable to wait until we met and would get tanked up at home first. Not surprisingly they got fed up with me turning up at the start of the night in that state and gradually left me one by one. That, coupled with being barred from all my local pubs, led me to drink even more at home.

I also had a tendency to phone people up at the end of a drinking session, even close friends and family, and subject them to the most appalling insults imaginable. Even my mother and sister were on the receiving end. The problem was I really could not remember anything the next day. I would have no recollection at all of anything I'd said or done. I was a complete Jekyll and Hyde character, which is probably why I got away with it for so long. When I was sober I would never dream of insulting anyone, least of all those close to me, but as soon as I was drunk I just lost all sense of reality and turned into a vicious monster. Robert Philip, writing in the *Daily Telegraph* after the 1997 Open, summed up my character perfectly when he said: 'Although he could fill cabinets with the trophies he won, he could empty entire clubhouses with his vocabulary. Humorous, welcoming and courteous in sobriety, his drunken alter-ego was a vicious-tongued boor.' I was never violent, never struck anyone. It was just my mouth that I couldn't control. Even now, several years later, I am deeply embarrassed when I think back to those dark days.

When people told me I had phoned them while I was drunk, and told me what I'd said to them, I would be horrified. I wouldn't recognise myself. I didn't believe I was capable of some of the things I was doing and saying until a girlfriend taped my phone call one night and gave it to my mother. She told me to listen to it to see the distress I was causing to people I cared about, but I just refused. I was too horrified and couldn't bear the thought of listening to the tape. I would remember walking into a bar at the start of the night then the next thing I knew I'd be lying in bed the next day, often soaked in my own urine, with a tremendous hangover. I would know I had been on yet another binge, but I would have no idea where or with whom. I would lie there appalled with myself and dreadfully ashamed. I would take the phone off the hook and refuse to go out because I didn't want to be told what I had done the previous night. I would be so full of guilt and remorse I would just lie there dreading meeting or speaking to anyone who'd seen me.

I would tell myself time and time again that I was finished with drinking. Each morning I would tell myself there would be no more sessions. I would decide that I would only have a couple of drinks instead, and I would often take my first pint thinking:

'I'll just have two or three to be sociable.' But it was impossible to stop at two or three. I was a binge drinker. I was like an animal tasting blood and wanted more and more. Some people regret taking 'that extra drink' at the end of a night, but it would be the first one I would regret. It sounds ridiculous, but the first drink would make me drunk. As soon as I had a taste for it I couldn't stop until I passed out. I would not touch a drop from Monday to Thursday, but by Friday lunchtime I would start to get twitchy as my longing for a 'hit' started to get the better of me. As soon as I took that first sip, that was it, I was hooked. I also had to drink the super-strength stuff because ordinary drinks just wouldn't have any effect. If I just had a can of regular lager it would be like drinking tea.

Eventually the near-constant feelings of guilt and the non-stop terror of who I'd insulted began to take their toll and I started to suffer from depression. I still kidded myself on that I wasn't an alcoholic because I wouldn't drink from Monday to Thursday. I thought alcoholics got drunk every day. That wasn't me. I was strictly a weekend only man and I never missed a day's work because of alcohol. Of course I was only fooling myself.

The morning-after feelings, when I didn't want to leave the house in case I bumped into someone who had been on the receiving end of my foul mouth the previous night, were becoming impossible to deal with. I knew that I had to stop getting so drunk, but what still hadn't dawned on me was that I could not even have one drink, because any time I did, that was it – oblivion. I certainly became suicidal and considered taking my own life on at least a dozen occasions. As stories of my behaviour came back to me I found it difficult to live with the shame I was bringing on myself and my family. Many times I thought about going to my car and connecting a hosepipe up to the exhaust, but I didn't have the guts to kill myself. I was too much of a coward to do that.

My behaviour was unforgivable and I can't blame the friends who wanted nothing more to do with me. One by one they washed their hands of me because of the way I treated them, and it's exactly what I deserved. How my family stuck by me I'll never know, but I will always be grateful for their love and support throughout the good times and the bad.

One person who had finally had enough, though, was my second wife Alison. I knew her from Cochrane Castle and we married in 1981. Alison's parents were members of the club and she also played a bit as well. Alison hardly drank at all and it must have been agony for her to watch someone she loved acting in such a self-destructive way. We split up in 1985 and it is a tribute to her patience that the marriage even lasted that long. I was a truly awful husband. We would frequently arrange to go out on a Friday or Saturday night but I would come home extremely drunk and barely able to speak. Eventually she got fed up and started going out with her own friends. I didn't care because I would be lying, passed out, on the couch. Alison tried again and again to tell me that I had a problem, but I just didn't listen to her. As far as I was concerned, my only problem was finding a pub near my house that would still serve me. It was obvious the marriage would fail if I didn't cut out the boozing but I just didn't care. The only thing in my life I cared about by this time was drinking. My craving for alcohol made me incredibly selfish and was the reason she left me. She just told me one day: 'Barclay, it's over.' I just accepted it. It was a situation where I either had to give up drinking or give up on my marriage. Well, frankly, there was no contest. Drinking meant more to me than anything else in the world but still I didn't see what was plain to everybody else – that I had a major problem. I still enjoyed playing golf but it was coming an increasingly distant second place in my list of priorities. The only reason I went to work was because I needed the money to feed my addiction.

I would have other girlfriends from time to time, but they would soon get fed up with me as I would turn up drunk for dates. The relationship would generally fizzle out pretty quickly, but again I wasn't bothered. I just thought someone else would come along the next week, and if she didn't then so what? As long as I could get a drink I didn't care.

I must have been a pitiful character to those who knew me. I must have come across as a sad, pathetic individual. Everyone could see that, at best, I was ruining my life, and, at worst, slowly killing myself. Everyone except me, that is. But my eyes were about to be opened.

For the rest of the 1980s my game was still in reasonable shape and I was picking up a few trophies, but there was no way back as far as the Scotland selectors were concerned. I don't blame them for that, in fact I think they were quite right to ban me. I still enjoyed playing tournaments, though, even if I needed a few drinks to help me get round. As the 1990s began I still hoped I would be able to redeem myself in the eyes of the selectors, but realistically I knew this was unlikely and I made no effort to change my lifestyle. I was still drinking as much as – if not more than – ever. They say every alcoholic has to hit rock bottom before they can start climbing out of the pit they have dug for themselves. Well, my nadir was just around the corner.

I had not played too well in the 1991 West of Scotland Open; a 72-hole tournament being held over a weekend at Renfrew. I finished about fifteenth and was not terribly impressed with myself. The tournament had been won by Andrew Coltart, now a Ryder Cup player who has had a good deal of success on the European Tour. After the presentation I was sitting with him and Dean Robertson, one of my closest friends and a player now doing well in the professional game. We'd had a couple of pints and were chatting away when Andrew decided to fill the trophy with whisky and shouted to me: 'There, get stuck into that Barclay.' Well, with an offer like that I didn't need a second invitation and got fired right in. That is the last thing I remember about the night. I got into a real state and woke the next morning filled with guilt and remorse once again. I had no idea what I'd said or done, but I was sure I'd been at my most offensive. The truth emerged over the next few days. First of all my caddie that day, Davie Roberts, told me that I had been in 'some state' and had offended everybody. He started to tell me exactly what I'd said and I just told him to stop, I couldn't bear listening to it. Then I got a phone call from one of the Renfrew committee members, a friend of mine called Colin Brown. He confirmed my worst fears when he told me I'd been at my most obnoxious and abusive. He said a number of people had been subjected to appalling abuse, including the teenage daughter of a club member. I knew how serious this was, and Colin, as a friend, was trying to help with the damage limitation. He told me to write a letter of apology to the members, the committee and the father of the girl. I did all this, and meant every word of my sincere apology, but I was pretty sure the matter would not be at an end.

Unfortunately for me, Renfrew had a match against Cochrane Castle that week and, although I wasn't playing, I was the main topic of conversation. The Cochrane Castle captain, David Dickie, was understandably alarmed to hear that a member of the club had acted in such an offensive manner, and a few days later I was summoned to appear before the committee. I knew I was likely to be banned from the club but, instead of doing the sensible thing and going along full of contrition in the hope of a lenient sentence, I did the worst thing possible and turned up drunk. I then stood in front of the committee and gave each of them, many of whom were friends, a piece of my mind. My behaviour was disgusting and the only surprising thing was that I wasn't banned for life. Later that night a member of the committee came to my house and slipped a letter through the door informing me that I was banned from Cochrane Castle for a year. They also suspended my handicap which meant I was unable to play in any tournaments. I was effectively out of the game – in more ways than one. I had two failed marriages, my family were at their wits' end and many of my friends had deserted me. I was drinking myself to death and now I couldn't even play golf. Finally, I'd hit rock bottom.

GORDON SIMPSON

Former golf writer and now Director of Communications with the PGA European Tour.

When I first started covering the Scottish golf scene in the 1980s I quickly heard various stories about Barclay and the things he was supposed to have said and done while drunk. But I can honestly say that I liked Barclay from the first time I met him. As a journalist, I found his jaunty demeanour very appealing and he was never anything less than courteous any time I interviewed him. He was also never afraid to speak his mind and would answer all my questions thoroughly and honestly. This included the first time I interviewed him after his ban from the game in 1991. Like everyone involved in the game I had known from tittle-tattle that Barclay had a bit of a drink problem, but I had no idea of the extent of it until then. As he discussed it with me I could not believe the total frankness with which he spoke. He did not hold back anything as he explained how his drinking had very nearly destroyed not just his golf career, but his whole life. I remember thinking at the time that I couldn't believe anyone would wish to bare their soul like that in a newspaper. I thought that if it was me, I would be a lot more reticent about the skeletons in my cupboard. That is, however, typical of Barclay. He is completely open and honest. He is ashamed of the way he has behaved in the past, but he is not ashamed of people knowing. Barclay is not a publicity seeker, but when asked for an interview about his drinking he was prepared to give it – and give it truthfully. Speaking openly is his way of dealing with what's happened and I have great respect for him because of that.

It was tremendous to see him get back on his feet over the next couple of years with his new wife, his new job and his new-found enthusiasm for golf. That's why the 1997 Open was so memorable for me. I remember an incredible feeling of exhilaration at Troon that year as I saw Barclay's name on the leaderboard at the end of the first day. For an amateur golfer to play in the Open and find himself leading the field must be like sticking a Sunday league footballer into the Brazil team to discover he's their star player. It was amazing to see how much he relished the whole occasion and I remember him telling me: 'I've got everything back on track now – my wife, my daughter, my golf and my job. Nothing can go wrong now.' The press conference that night was quite an eye-opener because although a few of the journalists there, like myself, knew about Barclay's past, there were an awful lot from around the world who didn't. As he told them all about his drinking and how he would win tournaments while consuming cans of lager on the way round, the American journalists in particular couldn't believe what they were hearing!

The last day was also very special. The reception Barclay received at the eighteenth hole had to be seen and heard to be believed. I don't think I have ever heard such cheering for someone who is not winning an event. It was the sort of welcome given to the likes of Jack Nicklaus or Arnold Palmer when they play a course for the last time. It made the hairs on the back of my neck stand up just being there to witness it all. It really was electric.

The life-threatening illness which was lurking just around the corner is a terrifying example of how cruel life can be. I was at the Quaker Ridge course in America a couple of weeks after the Open, covering the Walker Cup, and knew something was wrong with Barclay. Like everyone else, however, I had no idea it would be something as serious as cancer. I remember one of the practice days being quite hot, but by no means unbearable. Yet Barclay's shirt was soaked right through with sweat and he looked grey and sickly. Everyone else in the Great Britain and Ireland team was sweating lightly, but it was just pouring off Barclay. Like him, however, I just thought he must have some sort of virus. I couldn't believe it when he was diagnosed with leukaemia a couple of weeks later.

While he battled the illness his appearance changed greatly as his hair fell out and he lost an awful lot of weight, but, I'm glad to say, his personality didn't. He remained as frank as ever as he discussed the illness, and kept his sense of humour. Even doses of chemotherapy were not enough to stop his wisecracks.

Barclay's life seems to have been full of extremes; with his good times tremendous highs like the Open and the 1995 Walker Cup; and the bad times very deep lows such as the cancer and the drinking. Hopefully the worst is now behind him and the best still ahead.

FIVE

The Eternal Battle

It's amazing how the cold light of day – and sobriety – can change your view of things. When I woke up the next morning it dawned on me exactly what I had done and what it meant. Golf was the most important thing in the world to me. I had always felt as though playing the game was what I was put on this earth to do. Now, because of my stupidity, I'd been booted out of the club I loved and was honoured to represent, and told I could not play again for a year. I had been a member of Cochrane Castle since I was a child and had been awarded honorary life membership in 1980 after being selected for the St Andrews Trophy. If I went more than a couple of days without playing golf I would get withdrawal symptoms. A year seemed like a lifetime.

Talk about the morning after the night before. Only this time I didn't just have a hangover from the drinking. I had a second, bigger headache – what was I going to do about the downward spiral my life was heading in? My second marriage had broken up because of my drinking, I had lost most of my friends and now it looked as though my days as a golfer were numbered. My life was at a crossroads and a wrong turn now would spell disaster. Basically, I had two choices. I could ignore the advice of the few people who still cared about me and continue my self-destructive lifestyle until it killed me. Or I could finally listen to what they were saying and get help. It was a difficult choice because, like all alcoholics who refuse to seek help, I really didn't believe I had a problem.

At this time I was saving my extreme drinking sessions for the weekend and generally not drinking during the week because of work. This meant that I had a clear head for the first couple of days after my ban and I spoke to my mother and sister about what I was going to do. They urged me to go and see an old family friend, a doctor in Johnstone called Sarah Marr. I made an appointment to see her at her surgery on the Friday of that week, four days after disgracing myself at the disciplinary hearing at Cochrane Castle. I didn't know quite what I expected from Sarah because, although it was slowly beginning to dawn on me that I had a problem with my drinking, I certainly didn't consider myself an alcoholic. I really only drank at the weekend and, although I was prepared to admit I drank quite heavily, that didn't make me an alcoholic. Alcoholics were the tramps you would see lying in the street drunk on a Saturday afternoon, clutching a bottle of cheap whisky in a brown paper bag. I certainly was not one of them, and was in no danger of becoming one, I thought to myself, as I made my way to Sarah's surgery.

When I got there I explained that I had got myself into trouble with the golf club because of my drinking and didn't know what to do about it. I asked what she could do to help me. I knew she wouldn't just be able to give me a couple of tablets and say: 'There, you'll be fine now', but I hoped she could help, perhaps tell me how I could just enjoy a few pints without every drink turning into a mammoth session. Or maybe she would have a few tips on controlling my abusive mouth, which had got me into so much trouble when I was drunk. I certainly didn't expect what she told me. After I had gone through things with her she simply said: 'Barclay, I'm going to make a phone call right now, be ready to be picked up at your house at seven o'clock tonight.' I asked what for and she told me: 'You're going to be taken to a meeting.' I knew what this meant and protested: 'But I'm not an alcoholic.' Sarah simply told me: 'Just go to the meeting then phone me on Monday and tell me what you think.' This was the first of two occasions on which Sarah's prompt actions undoubtedly saved my life.

I heard the car pull up outside my house at seven o'clock as Sarah had said. I went down and found two men in the car. I introduced myself as Barclay and they said they were Davie and Stevie. They told me we were going to an Alcoholics Anonymous meeting in the Foxbar area of Paisley, a few miles from my home in Johnstone. All the way there I kept telling Davie and Stevie: 'I don't know why I'm going to this, I'm not an alcoholic.' Obviously they'd heard this all before; in fact they had undoubtedly used the same words themselves. They told me just to sit and listen when we got to the meeting and that I wouldn't even have to say anything unless I wanted to. I settled back in the car and got ready for what I expected to be a waste of an evening with a load of sad old inebriates who had nothing to look forward to in life but their next drink – nothing like me at all.

I would say it took fully ten minutes for me to realise just how much I had been kidding myself for years. As I sat there listening, expecting to be bored rigid by sorry tales of woe, it quickly dawned on me that, in many ways, I was no different from any of the people in that community hall. They were not a bunch of down-and-outs begging in the street for the price of a pint. They were just ordinary people with a drink problem. The stories they told made my difficulties with Cochrane Castle look pretty insignificant. That night I heard tales of hardship and desperation that beggared belief. I also heard stories of the dreadful way people had behaved because of alcohol: people who had stolen, been to prison, slept rough, turned to violence – all because of alcohol. Grown men who wet the bed at night because they were too drunk to wake up. And in every one of the stories I recognised a part of myself. As people spoke of the insults, the bed-wetting, the blackouts, the hallucinations, the failed relationships and the friendships which ended one by one, I knew I was one of these people. I realised that alcoholics weren't all unemployed, homeless drop-outs. I realised that alcoholics came from all walks of life. I realised these friendly, articulate people were alcoholics. Finally, I realised I was an alcoholic. Everything my family and few remaining friends had been saying to me for years, and which I had dismissed as a load of rubbish, was true. I also quickly realised that once you reached my stage there was no middle ground. It was too late for me to try to cut back on my drinking and say to myself: 'I'll just have a couple of pints on a Saturday night after golf.' That wasn't an option. It was obvious that the first drink is the problem for an alcoholic, and the only chance you had of staying sober was not to take it.

The tales people were telling, about the lengths they would go to in order to get a drink and the effects alcohol had on them, were truly terrifying. The most horrifying story that night was from a man in his 20s who used to suffer dreadful, alcohol-fuelled hallucinations. On one occasion he believed there were rats crawling all over him and he began to scream in terror. He tried to brush them off with his hands but it seemed there were too many of them, all over his body. So he grabbed a kitchen knife and started stabbing the rats. But, of course, he was plunging the knife into himself repeatedly. The surgeon who saved his life told him he had lost so much blood it was a miracle he survived.

After spending a couple of hours listening to stories like that I took a decision that changed – and in all probability saved – my life. I stood up in front of the couple of dozen other people there and said: 'My name is Barclay, I'm an alcoholic and I've just realised it tonight.' I told the gathering I was delighted to be there and grateful to be sober, but that I didn't want to say too much more that first night. One thing that had, however, become quickly apparent was that there is no point in an alcoholic realising he has a problem then simply saying: 'I'm never going to drink again.' It just doesn't work like that. Each day has to be taken one at a time. So before I sat down again I simply added: 'I'm not drinking tonight.' Everybody else in that room had been in the same position as me before and knew how hard it is to admit to yourself that you are an alcoholic, far less tell a roomful of strangers. They clapped and nodded and seemed genuinely pleased that I had taken what is an enormous and genuinely terrifying step.

After the meeting had ended I sat drinking tea with Davie and Stevie and talking about what had happened that night. They recalled what I had been saying in the car on the way there: that I wasn't an alcoholic and that it was all a big waste of my time going to this meeting with them. Now I had no choice but to admit to them that I was wrong. There was no question that my drinking was completely out of control. There was no point in kidding myself any more that I was just a social drinker, or even a heavy drinker. There was no point in mincing my words. I knew what I was now and I admitted it to Davie and Stevie again – I was an alcoholic.

As we talked, Davie told me that he was a regular at AA meetings, and the more we chatted, the clearer it became to me that my life was balanced on a precipice, and if I fell the wrong way then it would soon be over. I ended up going back to Davie's house in Linwood that night and stayed talking to him and his family until two o'clock in the morning. There were about ten members of his family in the house that night, including his wife Mae, sons, grandchildren and one of his daughters who was introduced as Letitia – or Tish for short.

We mainly talked about the meeting and I told Davie that I felt I had got a lot out of it; that I had a new picture of how my life was, as well as where it was going. It wasn't a pretty sight. I told him that I wanted to stop drinking, that I needed to stop drinking, but that I realised tomorrow was another day and there would be a lot of difficult times ahead. He asked if I wanted to go to another meeting the next night and I didn't hesitate to say yes. In some ways the evening in Foxbar had been one of the most horrifying, depressing nights of my life as I listened to the tales of tragedy – many of them self-inflicted – from my fellow alcoholics. In other ways, however, it had been hugely fulfilling as I realised the source of all my problems in life. Going to another meeting the following night certainly wasn't my idea of fun, but then neither was drinking myself into an early grave, which seemed the only other real option.

Davie knew of another meeting in the area the next night and he willingly agreed to come with me. There are AA meetings all over the place every night of the week, and for the next three months we would spend a couple of hours at one every night. It was the only way I could see myself staying off the booze. The weekends were particularly hard as I used to spend all week at work, desperate for Friday evening to come round so I could start my three-day benders. It didn't matter if I was playing golf because I would just shove some cans of lager into my bag before heading for the first tee. The meetings were especially important to me at the weekends as they gave me something to do other than drinking. Going to meetings and hearing other alcoholics describe the torture they had gone through, as a result of their addiction, and hearing how they were managing to fight the hugely powerful urge to have just one drink was an enormous inspiration. If they could do it, with everything they had been through, I knew I could too. And I was determined to do it. I owed it to my family, my friends – and most of all to myself. Listening to others at the AA meetings made me realise I was only inches from throwing my life away completely. If I had kept going the way I was I would have ended up jobless, homeless, friendless and probably disowned by my family. It would have been only a matter of time until I drank myself to death. The small matter of my golf ban seemed fairly inconsequential compared to all that.

After about three months I started to cut back slowly on the number of meetings I attended, to about five a week at first then, as the months went by, to fewer and fewer. Nowadays, I seldom go, though I admit I do still feel the urge to have a drink from time to time. Since that first meeting I have only drunk on about ten occasions, and the last was in 1997. Each time I was left feeling ashamed and determined not to fall off the wagon again. Hopefully, the occasion in 1997 will turn out to be the last. If I am finding it difficult I can still go to the AA meetings, or more likely chat to Davie, who has now been sober for more than 20 years. His invaluable help with beating my alcoholism is not the only reason I have to be indebted to Davie Muir, though, he also introduced me to my third (and last!) wife, his daughter Tish.

At the start, I would usually go back to Davie's house after the AA meetings, and Tish and I would just chat more and more. It was obvious that we got on well and she understood exactly what I was going through because she'd seen it before with her dad. She was very supportive and it was no time at all before we were talking about anything and everything, not just my drinking problems. I don't want to sound too corny, but it really felt as though we'd known each other for years. Within a couple of weeks of meeting we started going out together and the relationship just took off. My feelings for Tish were another incentive to stay sober. Davie's support and the AA meetings were crucial in my battle with the bottle, but it was meeting Tish which convinced me that my life was finally going in the right direction. If it hadn't been for her, I doubt if I would have been able to stay off the drink for too long. She was the best reason of all to stay sober and undoubtedly saved my life. Another reason came when we found out she was pregnant a few months later. We married at Johnstone Registry Office on 24 April 1992 and our daughter Laura-Jane was born less than four months later, on 13 August. By that time I was back playing golf – playing good golf – and it seemed as though my life was finally complete.

There is no doubt that my drinking caused my second marriage to fail, and as soon as Tish and I got together I was determined not to let alcohol ruin a new chance at happiness. She has always been patient with me if I have found it difficult and fallen off the wagon. Just a couple of weeks after we got together, we were out with one of her brothers and his wife. It was a Saturday night and we had gone out for dinner and I had about three or four pints. Nobody tried to persuade me not to, because their experiences with Davie meant they knew that is not the way it works with alcoholics. They just said: 'If you really want a drink, then have one.'

The next day I was furious with myself and thoroughly ashamed. I had not behaved badly, but I felt guilty about what I'd done, as if I had let down everyone who had helped me. I then started to think about my past and all the times I had been drunk. I was trying to think of any good times I'd had while drunk but there were none. I really couldn't come up with one experience which had been enhanced because I was fuelled with alcohol. I thought of all the tournaments I'd competed in – and the many I'd won – where I had gone out and played with my golf bag stuffed full of cans of lager that I would drink on the way round. Those were not times I could look back on with pride. Instead I was remembering them with disgust. It was hard to have any respect for myself if the only way I could play golf was to get drunk on the way round. It is no way to conduct yourself and the more I thought about it all, the more ashamed I became of the way I'd acted in the past. I also thought of all the trouble I'd caused, mostly for myself, and the hurt and upset I'd inflicted on people I loved, like my mother and my sister. I thought of the good friends I'd driven away who no longer wanted anything to do with me because of the appalling way I'd behaved, verbally abusing them while drunk. The ones who stuck by me through all that I can't thank enough, I don't know how they did it. As for the others who were understandably sickened by my behaviour, well, I can hardly blame them. I also thought of the times my mother Wilhelmina begged me to stop drinking. She stood by me through thick and thin and it must have been terrible for her to watch her only son boozing his life away. She would plead with me to stay off the drink, telling me: 'You're just such a different person when you're sober, you're a lovely man, but you're just horrible when you're drunk.' She had to put up with a lot. I can only imagine what it must have felt like to be stopped in the street time and again to be told: 'I saw Barclay last night, he was in a real state.' She must have been at her wit's end. It's lucky I didn't kill her with the stress I must have put her under. My sister Morag and her husband Bob tried desperately to help me, imploring me to stop drinking, trying to show me how I was wasting my life and hurting the people I cared for.

I also recalled all the times I would go to a pub to be told I was barred. When I protested and demanded to know why, I would be told that it was because of the way I had behaved the previous night, but I wouldn't even remember having been in that particular pub the previous night. Eventually I was barred from every pub in Johnstone – all 13 of them – which is some feat considering the reputation some of them had. Even hardened criminals would think twice before going into one or two of them.

I thought, too, about all the times I had wet my bed because I'd fallen asleep so drunk I couldn't control my bladder. I was a grown man in my 30s and I was still wetting my bed like a small child. It was disgusting. It was also a miracle I had never burned to death in my sleep. I lost count of the number of times I woke up to find bits of carpet or furniture smouldering away from lit cigarettes I had dropped as I passed out. I remembered the times when I would deliberately not eat anything all day so the booze would have a greater effect on me. I would literally starve myself, usually on a Friday, so I could get more blitzed at night. I was working on the shop floor at the Rolls Royce factory in Hillington at the time and I would be desperate for the day to end so I could get to the shop for my bottles of super-strength vodka and lager. It didn't matter what they tasted like, I just bought the strongest I could find because after a few mouthfuls I couldn't taste it anyway. I thought about the times I'd had to rely on my dog Jason to lead me home from the pub because I would have no idea where I was or how to find my own house. I also considered all the blackouts where I could remember nothing that had happened the previous day. I would remember walking into a pub then the next thing I knew it would be the following day and I'd be walking down the street in a completely different town with no idea of what had happened in between.

All these thoughts went through my mind that day after the night out with Tish and her brother and sister-in-law. I realised how pathetic my life had become because of alcohol and I knew I wanted to put it behind me. I had met a wonderful new woman, had proved to myself I could manage without a drink, even if it had only been for a few weeks, and I didn't want to risk throwing everything away again. I promised myself that was it; I would never touch another drop.

Anyone who has battled alcoholism will understand how difficult that sort of promise to yourself can be to keep, and I have to admit I was unable to. Since then there have been other occasions where I've been drunk, usually at the end of international golf competitions where the team has been celebrating, and most notably after the 1995 Walker Cup. Each time I was offered a drink, I knew I shouldn't take it but, without trying to make excuses, in that sort of atmosphere, with a group of team-mates, it is very hard to say no. Luckily my behaviour did not get out of control on any of those occasions, but each time I felt ashamed of myself the following day. Every time I did it I was just putting myself back to square one. Instead of being able to say 'I've been sober for six months', I could only say, 'I've been sober for a day.' Each time I had a drink I let down everybody who cared about me. I never lied or tried to cover it up and on each occasion told Tish what I'd done. She wouldn't be angry because she knew from her father's experiences how difficult it can be, but the worst part of all was the feeling that I might have disappointed her by drinking. It was not a feeling I enjoyed and on each occasion I was determined not to go through it again. I would speak to Davie and tell him I'd had a drink. It's important to be honest if you really want to stop drinking. After hearing my confession he would ask me if I'd had a drink that day. I would tell him no and he'd say: 'Don't worry, yesterday's history. Today is what counts.' I also had Laura-Jane to think of by now and any time I felt the need to drink I would try to imagine what she would think of me in later years if I was a drunk. It did not conjure up a pleasant image in my head and made me more determined to live a sober life.

An alcoholic never completely wins the battle, as even those who have been able to abstain from drinking for many years know they have to keep taking it one day at a time and that even one drink could lead them back to their old life. I can say, however, that I am *winning* my battle. That day at the Walker Cup in America on 10 August 1997, was the last time I had an alcoholic drink. Sometimes I feel the urge to have a drink and that is when I have to rely on the support of my wife and family as well as my father-in-law Davie, but fortunately those moments are becoming increasingly infrequent. The way my life is with Tish and Laura-Jane, along with the way I started to play golf after my ban was lifted, are enough to convince me that life is definitely better seen through sober eyes. I could easily find myself back in the twilight zone again if I gave in to just one of my urges to have a drink, or somehow convinced myself that I'm cured and can happily enjoy a sociable few pints with friends. It can be hard going if I am out with a couple of people who are having a drink and I am just sitting there with a glass of Coke or an orange juice. It is tempting to join them and have a pint, but I know I can't and I'm determined not to throw away all the hard work I've put in since 1991. I know exactly what it's like to have a drink problem and it is terrifying to think how close I came to ending up in jail, living on the street or even dead. Although I have come a long way, I know I'm not cured, you never are. I know I will always have to take one day at a time and that's what I'm doing.

DAVIE MUIR

Father-in-law

I'm sure a lot of fathers would not be too pleased if their daughter told them she was going out with an alcoholic. Even fewer would like it if she announced just a few months later that she was going to marry him. But that's what happened to me – and I could not have been happier. Barclay Howard became my son-in-law when he married my daughter Tish, but almost since we first met he has been like a son to me.

I remember vividly the day I went to his house to pick him up and take him to his first Alcoholics Anonymous meeting. Almost as soon as we shook hands he was apologising for wasting my time, telling me there was no point in him going to the meeting because he was not an alcoholic. He knew he had a bit of a problem with the drink, but thought that was as far as it went. It didn't take long at that first meeting for him to realise that his problem was a lot more serious than he had thought. People who knew Barclay had been trying to tell him for years that he had a major problem, but he just wouldn't listen to them. I didn't bother to try to tell him because there is no point. Alcoholics have to work it out for themselves and luckily Barclay did that just in time, probably, to prevent his life ending up in the gutter. That first night he listened to stories from all sorts of people from different walks of life, and saw parts of himself in each one. Then came the crunch. He either had to be honest with himself and confront his problem, or bury his head in the sand and carry on ruining his life. Bravely, he stood up and told a group of complete strangers that he was an alcoholic.

Since accepting that he has a problem, he has dealt with it with a great deal of courage and determination. That first night he came back to my house and we talked until the early hours of the morning. I helped him realise that, now he had admitted his problem, there was no quick cure. There is no point in somebody in the position Barclay was in simply saying: 'That's it, I'm an alcoholic but I'll never drink again.' It just doesn't work like that. He understood that it had to be one day at a time, and that if he fell off the wagon he had to be honest about it. Well, he has fallen off the wagon a few times since that day in 1991 and each time he has been honest about it and started his fight from scratch. He has now been dry since 1997 and I am immensely proud of the way he has turned his life around. Unless you have had a drink problem it is probably difficult to understand how difficult and what a huge achievement this is. In modern society it is extremely hard to avoid alcohol. There are adverts for all sorts of drinks everywhere you look, and so much social interaction revolves around pubs and licensed premises; every time Barclay walks into a golf clubhouse there are people drinking in a bar. The temptation is everywhere and it takes a strong man not to succumb. But Barclay has shown an impressive determination to rebuild his life. That's why it was so unfair when he was diagnosed with leukaemia.

I had gone to pick him up at Glasgow Airport when he flew back from the 1997 Walker Cup. I'd driven there in his car, as I usually did when he'd been away on international duty, and tried to hand him the keys so he could drive home as normal. He looked exhausted, however, and asked me to drive him home. I knew something was seriously wrong, but not for a second did I imagine he had something as terrible as cancer.

The way he dealt with his illness should be an inspiration to everyone. Yes, he had his down days, but who wouldn't under the circumstances? For 99 per cent of the time his spirit was unbreakable. I also think his battle with the drink helped him when he had cancer. I believe he said to himself: 'I'm not going to beat one illness just so another can kill me.' I have no doubt that all through his darkest days in hospital he kept using the thought of hitting a drive straight up the middle of the fairway once more as part of his motivation to get better. His other inspiration was of course his family, Tish and Laura-Jane.

It was obvious from the first time they met, after Barclay's first AA meeting, that he and Tish got on well. I have to admit, though, I didn't expect them to start going out together, but when they did I had no problem with it. Anyone could see how much they enjoyed being together and, anyway, I could hardly sit in judgement of Barclay having been a far worse alcoholic myself. It wasn't long before they announced they were getting married and again I was delighted. Barclay is one of the bravest and most decent people I've ever known and I'm proud to have him as my son-in-law. I know he would never let Tish and Laura-Jane down and that, as a father and grandfather, is all you can realistically ask for. He knows that he has behaved badly in the past because of his drinking and he is genuinely sorry about that. We all have to put the past behind us, however, and try to move on. Now he has beaten a second life-threatening illness and he deserves a run of good luck. I know it has been frustrating for him to have a number of setbacks while recovering from the cancer, and it is taking longer than he hoped to regain his full strength and fitness; but I just keep telling him to keep fighting. I know he is desperate to turn professional on the Seniors Tour when he turns 50 in 2003, and I'd love to see him give it a go. One thing is for certain, if he fails, it won't be for a lack of determination and sheer guts. He's got those in abundance.

SIX

Burning up the Fairways

When I was banned by Cochrane Castle I took a conscious decision to forget about golf until I sorted the rest of my life out. It was a difficult course of action for me to take as I had been playing almost constantly since I was a small boy, but I knew that if I wanted to straighten myself out and stop drinking then I would have to concentrate all my energy on that. Over the next few months I barely gave golf a second thought as I was going to AA meetings seven nights a week. As I began to believe I was winning my battle, however, my thoughts naturally began to drift back to the game. I was seeing Tish, I was managing to stay off the drink and my life seemed to be getting back on track. I started to realise how much I loved golf and how much I was missing the game. When they heard about the ban, a couple of friends had offered to take me to play at other courses, but I wasn't really interested. Cochrane Castle had suspended my handicap which meant I was unable to play in any competitions. I love the competitive nature of golf tournaments, and have never been keen on just playing social rounds of golf so I was well and truly bunkered, to use golfing parlance.

When the ban first came through I thought strongly about just saying 'stuff it' and never playing again, but after a few months without drinking I started to wonder how well I could play sober. After all, I'd won plenty of tournaments and even represented my country while being an alcoholic, so who knew what I would be capable of without a drink inside me? I spoke to Tish and my mother about it and it took about ten seconds flat for us all to agree I had to give it another go. I told them I was feeling a lot healthier since I had given up drinking and was keen to see just how good I could be. They told me they were right behind me and would support me all the way. It was all the encouragement I needed. I still had a few months left to run on my ban, but I set myself three goals:

1) I wanted to return to the Scottish amateur scene with a vengeance. I had won plenty of tournaments and broken course records in the past, but I wanted to go out and shoot scores that people wouldn't believe. I was determined to try and win every tournament I entered.

2) Representing your country is a huge honour for any golfer – any sportsman at all, in fact. I had been lucky enough to play for Scotland on several occasions, but had fallen foul of the powers that be because of my drinking. I knew that there were a lot of people who never wanted to see me in a Scotland shirt again, but I hoped that if I produced the goods on the course – and stayed sober – the selectors might be able to forgive and forget. It was asking a lot, but I was desperate to play for Scotland again.

3) The last of my goals presented far and away the biggest
mountain to climb. Despite all my tournament wins and
international honours, I had missed out on one thing: the
pinnacle of the game for any amateur golfer, the Walker
Cup. It is the Ryder Cup of the amateur game, fought out
every two years on alternate sides of the Atlantic. The only
difference is that Great Britain and Ireland provide the
Americans with opposition in the Walker Cup, compared to
a European team in the professional Ryder Cup. The rivalry
is just as fierce and the honour of being selected just as
great. Many leading amateurs even delay their entry into
the professional ranks in order to take part in this great
competition. I felt I must have been close to getting in the
team in the 1980s but, for whatever reason, hadn't quite
made it. I decided a Walker Cup place would be my ultimate
goal.

Instead of immediately heading for a driving range somewhere
to start smacking three irons, however, I decided to hang fire on
getting back to practising. I still had a few months to run on my
ban anyway, so I shocked everyone who knew the overweight,
chain-smoking, alcoholic Barclay Howard – and headed for the
gym. I was still working at Rolls Royce at this time and there
was a gym in the factory. I would go every day and do some light
weights and sit-ups, as well as using the exercise bike and
rowing machine. I worked hard at it, and as the weeks went by I
felt fitter and fitter. The flab also started to drop off and
eventually I lost about two and a half stones. By early 1992 I
looked and felt better than I'd done in years. The only thing left
was to start hitting golf balls again, and I was about to receive
some encouraging news to spur me on.

At the beginning of March the committee at Cochrane

Castle got wind of what I had been up to. I am sure that many people there thought I would just drink myself into oblivion once I got my ban, and I'm equally sure there were some who wouldn't care if I did, they were so glad to see the back of me. Luckily, though, I still had some friends at the club which I'd been so proud to represent all over the world for many years. One day I got a phone call from Robin Andrew, one of the club's past captains who I had always got on well with, asking me out for a meal. When we met he told me the committee had heard that I had been going to Alcoholics Anonymous and had stopped drinking. He said they had been hearing good reports about me and were considering letting me back into the club early. Robin added that the majority of the committee were on my side, but they needed my word that I had stopped drinking once and for all. Obviously, as an alcoholic, I could not say that categorically, but I could assure him that I was determined to do my best to stay sober and to get back to playing some serious golf. That was good enough for Robin, I just had to hope that when he reported back it would be good enough for the committee. A few days later I received a letter asking me to appear before them. I immediately thought back to my last summons when I turned up drunk, told everyone what I thought of them, and was promptly banned. This time though, there would be no question of me getting tanked up beforehand and things went a lot better for me. The committee told me they would be delighted to let me back into the club on 1 April – two months early and only a few days away.

As soon as I got my membership back I put my name down for the April Medal, which was held at the start of the month. It would be my first competitive outing in almost a year and I have to admit I was a bit nervous about how I would play. But I had a small secret which no-one in the club knew. After Robin had come to see me the previous month and it looked as though I was going to have my membership reinstated, I immediately set about practising again. I would go to a sports centre near my home every day and hit 100 balls, aiming through a set of rugby posts. I also kept my fitness regime going at the gym and this all meant that by the time I stood on the first tee for the April Medal I was in pretty good shape, despite not having played a round of golf in almost a year.

I knew some people were not pleased to see me back and, in all honesty, I can't really blame them. There were a number of people in that club to whom I had been extremely rude, arrogant and obnoxious during my drink-fuelled rants. It would be unreasonable to expect everyone just to forgive and forget being on the receiving end of my abuse, but once I had apologised — which I had — and was doing everything in my power to make sure it wouldn't happen again — which I was — there wasn't much more I could do about it. I just accepted that because of the way I'd behaved previously I would not be everyone's cup of tea at the club. It was unfortunate but it was the price I had to pay for my earlier misdemeanours. I certainly never considered joining another club. I had played on that course since I was a four-year-old boy and had no desire to join anywhere else. Also, part of my drive was the desire to show some of the people there that I could turn my life around and make a success of it. I wanted them to see the new me and admit, if only to themselves, that I wasn't just a drunken degenerate.

Anyway, I went out that day and shot a highly respectable 68. I was a tiny bit rusty, but I was definitely in good form and I decided the next few years would be dedicated to becoming the best golfer I possibly could. To do this I would have to become very selfish, as I believe any top sportsman does. I was not interested in playing social golf or bounce games with friends. I just wanted to spend my time practising and playing tournament golf. I wanted to be allowed to concentrate on my own game and didn't even play many of the matches for the Cochrane Castle team. I wasn't totally selfish though as I played three away matches towards the end of the season to help them stave off relegation.

I was still going to the gym and practising every day. Tish knew nothing about golf. She had never played and had no interest in it until she started going out with me, but she still encouraged me to give it everything I had. She knew how important golf was to me and she was also aware that if I was to stay off the drink then I needed something to focus on. So we struck a deal in 1992 that I could play as much golf as I wanted, as long as I didn't drink. I would go out every evening to practise and Tish would say it was fine. I had her blessing, as long as I didn't come home smelling of booze. It was exactly the kind of incentive I needed to stay sober.

I got myself a new coach, John Mulgrew. We just hit it off straight away and he was brilliant for my game. I trusted him completely and had total faith in whatever he told me to do. He would take me for a lesson any time I asked; sometimes I was seeing him four times a week if I was having problems. He was never too busy to help me and would always fit me in, no matter what else he had on. John certainly played a big role in relaunching my career.

Thankfully, all my hard work and John's advice was paying off. That season I won a few tournaments and felt that my game was improving slowly but surely. I was playing as well as I had done since 1984. I had won a few tournaments that year as well, but I had been drinking heavily then and I couldn't help thinking that a lot of my wins had been down to little more than pure luck. Now, however, everything I did on the golf course, every shot I hit, every putt I sank, was down to my own ability and hard work. Gone were the days of packing my bag full of cans of lager to take round with me so that I wouldn't get the shakes while putting.

Only once that year did I fall off the wagon during a tournament. It was the Scottish Strokeplay at St Andrews and Tish had come up for the weekend to support me. It was a 72-hole tournament – one of the most important in the amateur game – and at the end of two rounds I was lying third, and quite handily placed to make a charge on the last day. I was a bit nervous as I hadn't been back playing for very long but I knew if I could keep my game together I had a chance of winning. The only problem was that, despite all the hard work I had put in since my ban was lifted early, I still didn't have 100 per cent confidence that my nerve would hold without a drink. On the Saturday night I made an incredibly stupid decision and told Tish I was heading off to the shops to get a few cans of lager to take out with me on the course the next day. I reasoned that I was going to be nervous the next day and the only thing that would calm me would be a few drinks. I got through the morning round without touching a drop, but in the afternoon, as things got tight at the top of the leaderboard, I finally gave in to temptation. I drank three cans during the round, and my game just fell away. I took a nine at one of the holes and, after going into the final round challenging for the lead, ended up finishing in fourth place, several shots behind the winner. I had opened the first can on the third or fourth hole, and knew as soon as I took my first sip that it tasted awful. But the compulsion to keep drinking after taking my first gulp kicked in. As I headed home I was disgusted with myself for succumbing to temptation, but it is probably a blessing that my plan backfired. If the drink had steadied my nerves and I had gone on to win the tournament, then I would undoubtedly have convinced myself that it was the only way I could play well under pressure which would have been disastrous. I am sure my slip wouldn't have happened if I had been staying at home that weekend, because on the Saturday night I would have gone to an AA meeting where I always gained the strength to realise that I could cope with life without a drink. As we were staying in St Andrews, however, it wasn't really an option.

After I got home I went to see my father-in-law Davie, as I always did when I was having a problem or feeling the need for a drink. I told him what I had done and, as a recovering alcoholic himself, he understood exactly what I was going through. He didn't judge me or think worse of me or tell me how stupid I'd been. He just pointed out that people were beginning to respect me once more and that if I started drinking again I would lose that respect and never get it back. He also reminded me of how much self-respect I had now, compared to when I was drinking, and asked if I wanted to lose that. I knew I didn't and that was the last time I ever touched a drop of alcohol on the course.

Apart from that lapse at St Andrews, my golf was getting steadily better throughout 1992 and it reached the stage that each time I played I would stand on the first tee thinking that the opposition were going to have to play pretty well to beat me. I had a lot more self-respect and confidence and was enjoying my golf more than ever. Together with my more stable home life, thanks to marrying Tish and having Laura-Jane that year, I really had never been happier. Goal number one had been achieved. I was back playing tournament golf and playing it well. I had won a few events and felt I was one of the men to beat every time I teed up the ball.

It was now time to turn my attentions to my second target –

getting back into the Scotland team. As people saw the way I was playing that summer my name was being mentioned in some quarters for a possible international call-up but it never came. Perhaps it was felt that I still deserved to be punished for my earlier sins. Then again, perhaps that was fair enough. All I could do was keep playing well and keep my fingers crossed. I knew the standard of golf I'd produced in 1992 was good enough and, as the season ended, I told myself I would be back wearing Scotland colours the following year.

Colin Dalgleish was captain of the Scotland team then, and at the start of 1993 he told me that if I produced the goods on the course I would have as much chance of being selected as anyone. This was a huge relief as I had worried that I would continue to be punished for my past. But Colin was very fair. He knew what I had gone through and the steps I had taken to try to stay sober. He also knew how hard I was working at my game and how desperate I was to represent my country again. He just told me to keep myself going, produce the golf, and I would be back in the team. It was all I needed to hear. As the 1993 season approached I was already raring to go, but this was the final piece of motivation I needed to realise that all those long hours in the gym and on the practice ground had been worthwhile.

In May that year I was given an unusual opportunity to spend even more time working on my game: I was made redundant from Rolls Royce after 20 years, one of hundreds of workers laid off. I received fourteen thousand pounds in redundancy money but, as with anyone who loses their job, it was a worrying time for me and my family. I'm not sure that many people in my position would have done what I did next, though. Instead of heading down to the Job Centre or scouring the recruitment sections of the newspapers, I decided to spend the next two years playing golf full-time. I lived off the dole and my pay-off, but it was just something I felt I had to do.

I'm not sure how understanding most men's wives would be in a similar situation, but fortunately Tish was fantastic. If she had insisted I get another job then I would have done so, because nothing is more important to me than my family, but she knew how much this meant to me and didn't even attempt to talk me out of it. She said she was right behind me and somehow we would get by financially.

The freedom to play and practise any time I wanted took my game onto another level. Every morning and afternoon I would head up to the practice range at Cochrane Castle and hit hundreds of golf balls. I would practise my driving and long irons in the morning before heading home for lunch. Then in the afternoon I would work on my short irons, my chipping and my putting. I was also still going to the gym regularly and my game just kept on improving.

Again, I won a handful of tournaments and hoped I had done enough to make the six-man team for the European Championship. Unfortunately, the selectors didn't think I had. It was a blow, but instead of moping about it, I used it to motivate myself to try to get into the Scotland team for the Home Internationals in September that year. I had played in the Scotland teams which had won the event in 1981 and 1982, and it was a tremendous feeling which I was desperate to experience again. When the letter came through the door telling me I had been picked I was ecstatic. Despite Colin's reassuring words at the start of the year there was still a nagging doubt at the back of my mind that certain people wouldn't want me in the team no matter how well I played. To be selected was an incredible feeling. The icing on the cake was playing in the foursomes with one of my best friends and Cochrane Castle team-mate, Dean Robertson, in what was to be his last event before turning professional. Unfortunately, although I played all right, Scotland found the going tough at Royal Liverpool and we finished a disappointing third. But at least my disappointment over the result was eased by the knowledge that I had achieved the second goal I'd set myself a year and a half earlier. Now there was only one left to achieve – my, and every amateur's, dream of playing in the Walker Cup. It was due to be held next in 1995 at Royal Porthcawl, in Wales. I was determined to be there.

The following year, 1994, was a similar story to 1993 as my golf continued to get better and better. I was winning tournaments and I couldn't believe that I had wasted all those years drinking. I had done all right back then, but I wondered what I could have achieved if I had been sober and applied myself the way I was now.

My wins that year included the St Andrews Links Trophy, considered by many to be the biggest tournament in British amateur golf. It was the last of a run of four tournaments at the start of that season where I finished second, third, first and first. It is a gruelling event which involves negotiating a total of four rounds over the Old and New Courses at St Andrews, the home of golf. The highlight of the tournament was getting a rare birdie on the notoriously tough Road Hole in the last round. Lifting the trophy afterwards was, along with my Scotland debut, the biggest moment of my career up to that point. I said in an interview in the *Sunday Times* the following weekend: 'When the putt went in on the last hole it was like the whole world was lifted off my shoulders. In a way, it was frightening how much of a high it created, with people cheering and the history of the place.' It was an unforgettable feeling. Unfortunately though, my great achievement of scoring a rare birdie at the Road Hole was somewhat lost on my wife. I phoned

Tish to tell her I'd won the tournament and she was really pleased for me. But when I mentioned *that* birdie her reply was: 'That's great, dear . . . what's the Road Hole?' I guess that sort of thing is the price a man has to pay for marrying a non-golfer!

I was building up something of a following in Scottish golf ranks that year, possibly because of my past. I think a lot of people saw a bit of themselves in me. Maybe not as an alcoholic, but perhaps in the way they had faced other problems of their own, and they could draw strength from the fact I had beaten my demons and come back stronger than ever. In a feature in *The Times*, their golf correspondent John Hopkins even described me as a cult figure. He went on: 'He is small and chunky, moustached and gritty-voiced, witty and unemployed.' He also described me as having 'an old head on old shoulders'. I'm sure it was meant as a compliment!

Another memorable victory that season was the Newlands Trophy, a two-round competition at Lanark. The reason it sticks out is because it went to a marathon seven extra holes before I beat one of my best friends in the game, Graham Rankin. If we weren't talking afterwards it wasn't because we'd fallen out – we were just too knackered after playing 43 holes! I also broke an 18-year-old record in 1994 when I shot a 19-under-par 265 to win the Standard Life Gold Medal at Leven, one of the oldest trophies in the game. The previous record was held by my old Scotland team-mate and friend, Ian Hutcheon, which made it even more special.

The big amateur team event that year was the St Andrews Trophy, the biennial match where Great Britain and Ireland take on the rest of Europe. After the Walker Cup, it is probably the event that every amateur golfer in this country wants to take part in above all others. I had played in 1980 and was eager for the chance to sample the atmosphere again. I believed I was playing well enough to make the ten-man team but it was still a nerve-racking time waiting to hear if I would be selected. I'd had another good season, winning a string of tournaments and just had to keep my fingers crossed. When the team was announced with my name in it I knew I had well and truly put my past behind me. It was the final proof I needed that the golf world was prepared to forgive, if not necessarily forget, and it gave me huge personal satisfaction that I had bounced back from the depths of despair.

As the 1995 season got under way there was only one thing on my mind, the Walker Cup at Royal Porthcawl in September. My selection the previous year for the St Andrews Trophy meant I was obviously in with a good chance of making the team; as long as I could produce the goods on the fairways and greens. I was part of a 23-man preliminary squad selected at the end of the 1994 season to go down and have a look at the course. I loved the place immediately. The other guys in the squad were all great, the people in Wales were wonderful and the course and facilities were tremendous. The preliminary squad also got special coaching from that year's Ryder Cup captain Bernard Gallacher, but captain Clive Brown would only be naming ten players in the final team, so there was a lot of competition for places. I was determined to make one of the spots mine, but nobody was likely to get in on reputation and, as I said before, I knew I would have to come up with the goods during the season. I made my ambition clear when I said in an interview in the *Daily Record*: 'To be picked for a squad get-together at Royal Porthcawl at my age is tremendous encouragement. It's a huge bonus.' As part of my bid for selection I went on a fitness programme to lose weight. I was up around the 14 stone mark and wanted to shed a stone. 'I don't want to be a Charles Atlas but I want to get to around 13 stone,' I added in the interview:

'I've even stopped setting my alarm clock for 3 a.m. for my middle of the night snack!' I'm not sure if people thought I was joking about that or not.

I was able to keep my excellent form going into 1995, racking up a string of good results, although I was denied victory in the Scottish Amateur Championship, when Alan Reid beat me 3 and 2 in the semi-final. I felt I was playing well, though, and was confident I would be among Clive's ten names.

The side was due to be picked immediately after that year's European Team Championship, being held in Antwerp in July. Scotland had a very strong team consisting of myself, Gordon Sherry, Stephen Gallacher, Graham Rankin, Hugh McKibbon and Alan Reid. If this was to be the last chance to impress the Walker Cup captain then things could not have gone any better. We had a quiet build up to the event, which was a deliberate move on the part of our captain Colin Dalgleish, but this masked a steely determination to bring the trophy back to Scotland for the first time in ten years.

We started off in impressive style by leading the strokeplay qualifying before beating Wales 4–3 in a close first round tie in the matchplay. That put us into the semi-finals against France. A win by Stephen and Gordon in the morning foursomes meant we were tied at 1–1 going into the afternoon singles against the French. I then played my part by beating Jean Marc de Polo 3 and 2. Alan, on his 21st birthday, won comfortably, 4 and 3, while Gordon snatched his singles on the final green. With the match over, Graham and Stephen agreed to call their respective matches halved as we wrapped up the match 5–2 to set up a final against England.

We expected a close match, but in the end we steamrollered the Auld Enemy 6–1 to be crowned kings of Europe. We got off to the perfect start by winning both the morning foursomes.

Gordon and Stephen beat Lee James and Colin Edwards 4 and 3 while I teamed up with Graham to defeat Gary Harris and David Howell 3 and 1. In the afternoon singles I hit great form to bury Gary Wolstenholme 4 and 3 with a string of birdies, while Gordon beat the English champion Mark Foster on the last green, giving him a maxium six points out of six for the competition – a tremendous performance. Alan also won his tie with Lee James by one hole, while Graham and Stephen halved their matches. Afterwards, captain Colin Dalgleish described the win as: 'one of the greatest days I have ever been involved with in Scottish golf'. I know what he meant. Colin added: 'Right from the start we proved we were the best team here, winning the strokeplay qualifying so well. Then we had to carry the mantle of tournament favourites right through the matchplay stages, but we did it superbly. We had tough times against Wales and France but we showed the character to come through and the final was probably our easiest game of the three. But it is difficult not to do well with six such great players and six who get on so well and pull so much for each other.'

Our triumph had also put all the Scottish lads right in the spotlight for the final Walker Cup selection meeting taking place that night. Most people were tipping myself, Gordon Sherry, Stephen Gallacher and Graham Rankin all to make it. I just hoped they were right.

The R&A (Royal and Ancient Golf Club of St Andrews) were due to post the letters out to the chosen team members the following Wednesday and I was up at the crack of dawn waiting for the postman to arrive. Most people reckoned I had easily done enough to get in, but I wasn't taking anything for granted until I saw it in front of me in black and white. When I heard the thud of mail through the letterbox I dashed to the front door and saw the familiar R&A symbol on the front of an envelope. I thought that was it, I had done it, but then I remembered that the reserves would also be sent letters, so I tore the envelope open. Only then was I able to relax and celebrate as I read the letter informing me of my selection for that year's Walker Cup match against the USA. It was a fantastic feeling as I realised that all my hard work had paid off. The only hard bit now was having to wait two months for the competition to begin. At the time it seemed like an eternity away, but I just had to make sure I kept playing, and playing well. The last thing I needed now was for my game to let me down at the biggest moment of my career. I was desperate to do well. Great Britain and Ireland have had a poor record in the Walker Cup, winning just three times before 1995 since the competition's inception in 1922. I reckoned that this year, however, we had a very strong team and, with home advantage, really believed we were good enough to beat the Americans; despite the presence in their team of a young man by the name of Tiger Woods.

The prediction that four Scots would make the team on the back of our European Team Championship triumph proved accurate with Stephen, Gordon and Graham also getting in. We were joined by four Englishmen: Mark Foster, Lee James, Gary Wolstenholme and David Howell, along with two Irishmen in Padraig Harrington and Jody Fanagan. The only slight disappointment was there were no Welshmen picked to play in their homeland.

In the days running up to the event I could barely sleep for my excitement. It was hard to believe that, just four years earlier, I had been an alcoholic heading for a life in the gutter and was banned from the sport. Here I was, now about to fulfil my ultimate ambition by representing my country in the greatest event in amateur golf. It was unbelievable.

I travelled down to Wales with Graham Rankin and we were so excited that we resembled two children being allowed out to the park together on their own for the first time. When we got there and saw the TV cameras being set up we knew this was going to be the biggest weekend of our lives. Even on the practice days there were large crowds of spectators and the atmosphere was amazing. I was getting a buzz from being there that I'd simply never known before in my life.

The Americans were favourites, largely because of their record in the competition, but we knew that if everyone played to their potential, and with the right team spirit, we had a good chance. All the Scots were convinced the team spirit we had built up a couple of months earlier in Belgium had contributed greatly to our win there. Graham Rankin said after Antwerp: 'It was just incredible, I have never come across team spirit like it. We were pulling for each other so much that as soon as you were finished on the eighteenth you would quickly shake hands with your opponent then run over to see how the other lads were doing.' It was a team spirit we felt it was crucial to replicate if we were to give ourselves the best possible chance to win at Royal Porthcawl. Gordon Sherry also summed up the general mood in the Great Britain and Ireland camp in an interview a few days before the match started. He said: 'The Walker Cup is everything I have ever wanted in the amateur game. On the day anything can happen. If we play well we'll beat them, it's as simple as that. We don't need to fear anyone. I would happily lose my matches if it meant the team winning. If we won, people would look back and see it was GB and Ireland that had won in 1995, not the individual players.' That was exactly the sort of collective, play-for-the-team, attitude we all needed to find if we were going to win. Stephen Gallacher was more bullish with his prediction. He said bluntly: 'The main thing is to win. It would be easy to say "Right, that's me in the Walker Cup" and be satisfied with that, but for me it's not the taking part, it's the winning. We are as good as any of these guys, we have winners right throughout our team, we should just get dug in. We shouldn't be overawed by it.' While I admired Stephen's confidence and agreed with his sentiments I decided to be slightly less forthright with my pre-match quotes. I simply said: 'You don't have to play like a superstar. If we play our normal game, we'll get a result.'

In the days leading up to the start of the battle most of the talk in the media and among golf fans centred around two of the players taking part: Woods for America and Sherry for us. He might still have been an amateur back in 1995, but everyone in golf knew all about Tiger Woods. He had been singled out as a star of the future when he took just 48 shots over a nine-hole course when he was just *three* years old. As he prepared to turn professional he was being tipped as a superstar and his achievements in his pro career to date have certainly lived up to that billing. Gordon Sherry, a 6 ft 8 in. gentle giant, was being touted as our Tiger Woods, particularly after finishing fourth at that year's Scottish Open – the best performance by an amateur in European Tour history. Stars like Jack Nicklaus, Tom Watson and Greg Norman had all tipped him for the very top. On the eve of the Walker Cup our captain Clive Brown said of Gordon: 'I want him very much to lead the side. I see him as having tremendous experience and confidence to which others in the team can look.' Sadly, he has yet to fulfil his potential and found the transition into professional golf a whole lot tougher than Tiger. But that weekend in Wales in September 1995 the Tiger was well and truly tamed by Gordon as he spearheaded a glorious team effort.

By one of those twists of fate which make sport so

enthralling for players and spectators, Gordon and Tiger were drawn against each other in the opening morning's foursomes. The Scot was partnered by countryman Stephen Gallacher – the pair had won their three matches together in our successful European Team Championship campaign a couple of months earlier – while the American teamed up with the highly-experienced John Harris.

Before a ball was even struck, however, the first morning got off to a curious start when one of the American team, a player now finding success on the US Tour, Notah Begay III, turned up at the course wearing what appeared to be war paint on his face. He assured everyone it wasn't, adding: 'I'm not going to kill anybody.' He is a native American and explained that he always rubbed red clay on his cheeks when competing, a tip given to him by his mother. He had another curious idiosyncrasy in that he could putt right or left-handed, depending on his position on the green. He explained: 'A right-to-left putt I hit right-handed and a left to right putt I hit left-handed. Basically the ball is always breaking back towards me that way and I'm standing underneath it slightly.' Interesting. Once we'd been assured that he had not packed a tomahawk in his bag we were ready to go and the 35th Walker Cup was under way.

The Sherry v Woods foursome was the first match out that Saturday morning and it appeared that we might have been underestimating the power of the Tiger as the Americans scored an easy 4 and 3 victory. Things had started promisingly enough when they three putted to hand our boys the first hole. It was the last time Gordon and Stephen would have their noses in front. A wild drive by Stephen cost them the second hole, then, when Gordon sent an uphill putt way past the fourth hole, the Americans took a lead they never relinquished.

Clive paired me with Graham for the foursomes that day and

neither of us could wait to get going. We decided that I should hit the first tee shot, but as I stood over the ball, I swear I had never been so nervous in all my life. I was shaking like a leaf and wondering why anyone in their right mind would want to put themselves through this. Fortunately I hit my drive okay and sent it up the right side of the fairway. Unfortunately things didn't go very well for us after that. We lost the first four holes to give us a near impossible task against Begay and Tim Jackson. We mounted a bit of a comeback but, frankly, never really played well enough to give ourselves a chance and they deserved their 4 and 3 win. Despite the rather dismal Scottish contribution to the morning's play, we still looked like going in at lunch locked at two points each. Our Irish pairing of Padraig and Jody were on top form, hammering Kris Cox and Trip Kuehne by the biggest margin of the morning, 5 and 4. All eyes were then on Mark Foster and David Howell who were three up with four to play against Alan Bratton and Chris Riley. But a series of poor shots over those last four holes let the Americans back in. First, David found a bunker off the tee at the long par four fifteenth, and Mark could do no better than find more sand 70 yards further up the fairway. But they were still two up with three to play and, we reckoned, would have a point in the bag. At the next hole, however, David left his approach shot short. Mark got the ball to nine feet from the pin with his next shot, but David missed his putt and in a matter of minutes what had seemed like a virtually unassailable lead was looking perilous. David made amends on the seventeenth by sinking a nerve-racking seven foot putt to keep the one-hole lead going up to the last. But three putts by the Brits on the final green allowed the Americans to halve the match and lead 2½–1½ after the morning foursomes. The afternoon singles was to be another story.

All the spectators had been hoping the draw would throw up a Sherry v Woods clash in the singles, but although they didn't get the match they wanted, they saw both players in memorable matches, for different reasons. Gordon's singles against Begay was the first match out that afternoon, and he put his foursomes disappointment behind him to show why we were all expecting great things of him. He was simply brilliant as he shot a four under par round to put Begay – and his clay-stained cheeks – to the sword. But the performance of the day undoubtedly came from Gary Wolstenholme who beat the supposedly unbeatable Tiger Woods in a thrilling contest. Gary had started off superbly and was probably the only person in Wales that day who could believe what was happening as he found himself three up after the first four holes. But Woods showed the fighting qualities which have made him such a fantastic champion by battling back to be all square with just two holes to play. He then had a three foot putt on the seventeenth green to take the lead but, incredibly, missed it to bring the whole match down to the eighteenth. Amazingly, Woods pulled a nine iron approach out of bounds, which left Gary just needing a par to win the hole. He didn't let us down. It was a tremendous win and Gary's comments afterwards showed why his confidence never faltered, even as Woods pegged back his early lead. 'I wanted to play Tiger because I'm a showman and I wanted the attention and the backing of the crowd,' he said. He certainly got it. Gary's win over Tiger gave us a lift far bigger than the one point it gained for the team. To read the press coverage in the run-up to the match you would have thought that Woods was some sort of golfing god who was simply unbeatable. Gary's brilliant win shattered that myth and gave us all that final piece of self-belief we needed if we wanted to lift the Walker Cup.

Stephen, Mark and Padraig also recorded wins, over Tim

Jackson, Buddy Marucci and Jerry Courville Jnr respectively, while I halved my match with Alan Bratton after a much-improved performance. Only Graham Rankin and Lee James lost, both by only one hole, to give us a 5½–2½ 'win' in the singles and a 7–5 lead over the Americans at the end of the first day, all of which set us up for one of the most memorable days of my life.

Graham and I were left out of the foursomes line-up the next day, so we spent the morning charging around all over the course supporting the boys who were playing. Watching a match like that is probably even more nerve-racking than playing because you feel so helpless. You are desperate to contribute something and want to hit every shot, but in reality all we could do, other than cheer and encourage, was hand out dry towels to the guys as the match was being played in torrential rain.

Although we started the day with a two point lead, no one was under any illusions about how much hard work lay ahead if we were to lift the Walker Cup for only the fourth time in 35 matches. Things were made harder as Gordon and Stephen lost the opening foursomes to Alan Bratton and Chris Riley, 4 and 2. But David and Mark restored our two point lead with a 3 and 2 win over Kris Cox and Trip Kuehne. Gary and Lee suffered a heavy 6 and 5 defeat by Buddy Marucci and Jerry Courville, but our Irish pair came up trumps for the second day running as the Tiger was tamed once more. Padraig and Jody played magnificently to beat Woods and John Harris 2 and 1 to split the foursomes 2–2 and leave us 9–7 in front – just 3½ points from victory – going into the final eight singles.

In the afternoon the Americans put their star player, Woods, and their most experienced campaigner, John Harris, in the final two matches; obviously hoping they would have the edge at the end of the match if they could make up the two point deficit

Left: I'm not looking too svelte as a 15 year old as I try to get out of bunker trouble during the West of Scotland Boys Championship at Douglas Park in 1968.

Below: Looking angelic as a 16 year old at the Scottish Boys Championships in 1969 where I lost to Robert Fyfe in the semi-finals at the first extra hole.

Above: I've just won the Cumbrae Cup at Millport during the 1970s. Unfortunately for me, like many golf tournaments, it was sponsored by a whisky company. My prize bottle was probably empty by the time I got home. © Walter Kerr, Millport

Below: 1978 was a great golfing year for me and here I am with some of my trophies. Unfortunately, I had another love by now – booze.

Above: The victorious 1995 Great Britain and Ireland Walker Cup side before battle commences at Royal Porthcawl. *Standing*: Padraig Harrington, Mark Foster, Gary Wolstenholme, Gordon Sherry, Stephen Gallacher, David Howell. *Seated*: Jody Fanagan, Graham Rankin, captain Clive Brown, myself, Lee James. © Ian Stewart.

Below: With 'The Animal', Graham Rankin, looking tense during our foursomes against Notah Begay III and Tim Jackson at the 1995 Walker Cup. © Ian Stewart.

Above: Blasting out of a bunker during the 1995 Walker Cup.
© Ian Stewart.

Right: Looking concerned as my 25-foot putt on the last green against Alan Bradley in the 1995 Walker Cup trundles towards the hole.
© Ian Stewart.

The putt's dropped, the crowd's gone wild and I'm feeling a mixture of
relief and delight. It left Bradley with a 15-foot putt to halve the tie.
© Ian Stewart.

Above: The greatest moment of my career and a rare moment for British and Irish golf as we get our hands on the Walker Cup in 1995. © Ian Stewart.

Right: I've got tears in my eyes after rolling in my putt on the eighteenth green on the last day of the 1997 Open at Royal Troon. Behind me is my caddie and close friend Ian McCosh. © Brian Stewart.

Left: Shaking hands with American Tommy Tolles on the last green at Troon. A true gentleman who helped ensure this was one of the best days of my life.
© Brian Stewart

Below: With my biggest fan, my daughter Laura-Jane after the final round of the 1997 Open.
© Brian Stewart.

Above: Receiving the
Silver Medal for
best amateur at
the 1997 Open.
© Brian Stewart.

Right: With Tish and
Laura-Jane in
September 1998 on
my first day home
after a year in
hospital battling
leukaemia.
© Ian Stewart.

early on. However, their captain, Downing Gray, clearly hadn't banked on the unbelievable performances produced by the first British and Irish players out. Once again Gordon Sherry was asked to lead us out, and once again he produced the goods. He was involved in a thrilling match with Chris Riley. Gordon was two up after six holes but then found himself in bunker trouble at the fourteenth and fifteenth to be pulled back to all square. They halved the next, but then Gordon rose to the occasion at the last two. The seventeenth is a par five and Gordon played a beautiful approach shot to leave him with an eight foot birdie putt. Then Riley played a near perfect chip to guarantee a five and increase the pressure on Gordon. If he sank it, he would be going up the last, one up with at least half a point guaranteed. If he missed, then Riley could still win the match on the eighteenth green. But Gordon's nerve didn't falter as he coolly rolled it in.

Afterwards he admitted the putt was: 'the most important I've ever made'. *The Times'* golf correspondent John Hopkins described Gordon's reaction beautifully when he wrote: 'It was a big putt and the Scot marked it with his trademark lunge – fist clenched, teeth bared, right leg forward, like a fencer going in for the kill.' But he still had a lot to do at the last to ensure a point. Once more his nerve held as he fired a 160 foot approach to within three feet of the pin. Again John Hopkins was in full flow as he described how the ball pitched 'into the putting surface, juddered viciously to a halt as an aeroplane does when landing on an aircraft carrier, and stopped three feet from the flag.' When Riley missed his putt from ten feet he sportingly conceded Gordon's to give us the first singles point of the day. The scenes were amazing as Gordon was embraced by his dad Bill and captain Clive on the last green.

Despite being in the third match out, Stephen Gallacher was

the second to finish, with a brilliant 3 and 2 win over Trip Kuehne. Stephen came out of the blocks at top speed and was three up after eight holes. He then won the fourteenth to go four up and, despite a late rally from Kuehne, held on for victory. The second match out saw David Howell involved in a nail-biter with Notah Begay III, war paint and all. David won the first four holes, but then watched as Begay slowly clawed back the lead. David then found himself in trouble in a bunker at the sixteenth but played a peach of a wedge to within just a few inches of the hole to ensure he kept his lead. A four foot putt at the seventeenth then made sure of a 2 and 1 win. Amazingly, it also meant we had won the Walker Cup, because just at that moment Jody Fanagan went dormie three – three up with just three holes to play – on Jerry Courville to guarantee a half point and ensure that we had reached the magical 12½-point mark. He then halved the sixteenth to post a 3 and 2 win anyway, but not too many of the 10,000 spectators cared by that stage. The Walker Cup would not be going back across the Atlantic when the Americans left next day and that was all that mattered. It wasn't all that mattered to the players, however, because, although the Walker Cup had been won, there were still four matches out on the rainswept course – mine included.

I went out fifth against Tim Jackson and played pretty solidly to secure a half point from a match that was always tight. Mark Foster also halved with Buddy Marucci, although Padraig Harrington and Gary Wolstenholme lost to John Harris and Tiger Woods respectively. The Americans' plan of putting their strongest players out last had backfired. Although Woods and Harris did the business, it was too late to turn the match and Great Britain and Ireland were worthy 14–10 winners. The feeling was just awesome. I have never known anything like it. The 1997 Open at Royal Troon a couple of years later was an amazing experience, but I have never known anything like that day at Royal Porthcawl. Players were dancing, and Tish and my sister Morag had also travelled down to Wales to watch. I could barely remember ever being happier. The reactions of all the British and Irish players, and the sportsmanship of the Americans, was hugely memorable.

David Howell, whose birdie at the sixteenth against Notah Begay III had secured victory, said: 'It was the biggest putt I have ever made – by far. It's just brilliant. I can't believe it. The whole weekend has been marvellous, just incredible, the highlight of my life.' I knew exactly what he meant.

For our non-playing captain, Clive Brown, a Welshman, the occasion was made even more special by winning it in his home country. 'I am speechless,' he said immediately afterwards, before proving he wasn't by adding: 'It is a dream come true. It was a dream to be here in the first place but to win the Walker Cup here in Wales is something I never thought would happen to me, or in my lifetime. We holed the putts that mattered. It was down to confidence and the ability to take the pressure. That was the difference between the teams. The crowd was also instrumental in getting us into the right frame of mind. They were fantastic.'

The US captain, Downing Gray, was graceful in defeat, paying tribute to the way we'd played over the weekend. 'The British guys earned it, they earned everything they got,' he said. 'They played wonderful golf in one of the most competitive Walker Cup matches ever. I am proud of them and I am proud of my guys. It was a wonderful exhibition of amateur golf at its finest.'

Stephen Gallacher, who was just 20 at the time, said: 'It is the greatest moment of my life.' Jody Fanagan, the Dubliner who had been magnificent in winning all three of his matches, joked that the competition had put years on him and, referring to the 19–5 drubbing handed out by the Americans in 1993, added: 'There was a lot of pressure on us after the result of two years ago but we've answered all our critics. This used to be called the Walkover Cup because of the way the Americans dominated it, but not any longer.' Fellow Irishman Padraig Harrington, who has since achieved great success on the European Tour and played in the Ryder Cup, paid tribute to the tremendous team spirit we had built up. He said: 'There was something about this team, something different. I just felt all along that we were going to win.'

My only regret about the whole weekend is that I drank during the celebrations on Sunday night. There was a lot of champagne in circulation and when I was offered a glass I found it impossible to say no. I knew that I shouldn't even take one drink because it is impossible for me to stop there. That night was no exception. I started drinking heavily and ended up in a real state. Fortunately, my behaviour didn't return to the level of the 1980s and, somehow, I got through the night without offending anyone. However, as I travelled home the next day, I was ashamed that I had given in to temptation and thought of all the hard work I'd put in over the previous four years. I didn't want all that to just go to waste and was determined that would be the last time. It turned out not to be, but at least the occasions were getting fewer and farther between.

When I got home to Johnstone on Monday night I was still on a high which would last for weeks. I also had another reason to be pleased: I was starting a new job the next day in the customer services department at the golf club manufacturers John Letters. I was going to work in the offices at Hillington, Glasgow, and it was a dream job for somebody like me. Tish had been incredibly understanding after my redundancy from Rolls

Royce, and had supported me as I played golf full-time. Now the two years we had agreed were up, I had achieved everything I'd set out to and – more importantly – we were skint, so it was time to get back to work.

As 1996 came round I was still elated about the Walker Cup and couldn't wait for the season to start so I could get back to playing competitive golf again. Although I had achieved my biggest goal in the previous year, I started to think about the future. The next Walker Cup would be in 1997 in America and, while quite a few golfers have played in one, not many have played in two. So, with Tish's blessing, I decided to aim for that. But my more immediate target for 1996 was to make the four-man Great Britain and Ireland team for the Eisenhower Trophy, the world cup of amateur golf, which was to be held in Manila that year.

When the season got under way it seemed like everything I touched turned to gold. It was my most successful year ever and I just couldn't stop winning. I was hitting the ball so well and winning so many tournaments that I just wanted to play in everything I could. Out of my first 12 tournaments I won eight and came second in the other four. I worked out that I was 57 under par for the 12 events and had just one over par round – ironically at Cochrane Castle. It was actually getting to the stage where I had too many trophies and medals in the house for me to handle. Also, my insurers were getting a bit nervous about all the silverware I was collecting.

About midway through the season I was picked again for the Great Britain and Ireland team to take on the Rest of Europe in the St Andrews Trophy at Woodhall Spa. We were up against the best amateurs on the continent and I simply played out of my boots as we cruised to a comfortable victory. I picked up three and a half points out of a possible four and was starting to wonder if I was dreaming. Tish was right behind me, encouraging me to keep playing and practising, and Laura-Jane was doing great as well. Life simply couldn't get any better.

After the St Andrews Trophy, my next stop was Sweden where I played superbly to finish second in the European Individual Strokeplay, just one shot behind the winner. All in all I won 11 tournaments that year – including the Scottish Strokeplay Championship. That win gave me a lot of confidence as I headed down to the Royal St George's Course in Kent for the British Amateur Championship. Sadly, my golden streak finally ended when I lost in the quarter-finals to England's Colin Edwards by one hole. But my close friend Craig Watson was going well and had made it into the semi-finals so I decided to stay on and caddie for him. Ironically his semi-final was against Edwards and he gained some Scottish revenge by beating him by one hole to set up a final against Trevor Immelman over 36 holes. At the end of the first round, Craig was two down and a bit downhearted, but I knew he was good enough to win and even told Steve Ryder so in a live TV interview before the start of the second round. Craig didn't let me down and triumphed 3 and 2. But, while I had enjoyed contributing a small part to his success, I knew caddying wasn't for me and, as we headed back to Scotland, I was already looking forward to the rest of the season's golf.

Fortunately the Great Britain and Ireland selectors decided I had done enough to make the team for the Eisenhower Trophy along with fellow Scot Mike Brooks, the Tiger-tamer from the previous year's Walker Cup, England's Gary Wolstenholme, and Keith Nolan from Ireland.

We were due to play in the Hong Kong Amateur Championship the week before the Eisenhower to get us used to the hot and sticky conditions we'd be experiencing in the

Philippines. The tournament was held on an excellent course there called Clearwater – and I spent most of it gasping for water, the heat and humidity was so great. Keith pipped me by just one shot to take the title, but with a British and Irish one-two we looked in pretty good shape to take on the best amateurs in the world.

Hong Kong was a wonderful place, but I was shocked when we reached Manila. The level of poverty was unlike anything I had ever experienced before. There were beggars everywhere, many of them children, and a high level of homelessness. It seemed that thousands of people were sleeping in nothing more than shacks, or even under hedges. The fear of crime was evident from the fact that there were armed guards everywhere; even on the golf course. On the first practice day we were loading up the bus when we were told to take our clubs and bags on board with us instead of putting them in the luggage hold underneath. When we questioned this it was explained to us that there was a chance the luggage compartment would be broken into when we stopped at traffic lights.

The sheer poverty was brought home to me by my caddie; a local teenage girl who lived with her family in a tin shack beside the golf course. Because of the intense heat there were stalls every four holes selling food and drinks. Each time I bought myself a bottle of water I would get her a drink and a cake which she would always put in her bag. After a while I noticed that she didn't take them out to eat or drink and I asked her why not. She told me she would be taking them home for her family to share at night. Despite the obvious lack of money, she was always immaculately turned out and extremely polite and well-spoken, as was everyone we came across in the Philippines. They were lovely people dealing with problems and living conditions which made my battle with the bottle look like a breeze.

The competition went all right for us and we finished seventh out of nearly 30 teams – a pretty decent performance – and I finished top Brit in the individual standings at 15th. Realistically, the conditions were probably just too much for us to have a good chance of winning. I wasn't joking when, after shooting a first round 67, I told the press lads: 'I've cooked chickens in cooler ovens than the temperature out there.' Getting back to the air-conditioned hotel each night was a blessed relief.

I gave myself two targets in 1997: making the Walker Cup team again and playing in the Open at one of my favourite courses, Royal Troon. I was desperate to help Britain defend the trophy we'd won so memorably at Royal Porthcawl, although I knew taking on the Americans on their side of the Atlantic was quite a different proposition. As for the Open, I had tried to qualify once before, in 1982, and failed miserably. But I was hopeful that if I made it through qualifying – no mean feat in itself – I could acquit myself adequately.

First though, I was taking part in that year's European Team Championship at Portmarnock in Ireland. Scotland advanced comfortably to the final where I made a tactical blunder by asking to be dropped for the singles. I had been playing well all week, but thought it would be good for team spirit if I was left out of the singles, as each of the other players had been left out at one time or another during the competition. Well, it might have helped the team spirit but it didn't help the result as the Spanish beat us 4–3. I was furious with myself and even Peter Benka, who was chairman of the Walker Cup selection committee, asked me why I'd done it, saying it was madness as I was the best player in the team. I decided to chalk it up to experience.

Immediately afterwards the Walker Cup team was picked for

that year's match at Quaker Ridge. I was confident I had done enough to make it, but it was still a relief to get the news officially. Although I was once again itching to take on the Americans, I had another pressing engagement to take care of first – qualifying for the Open.

I was a much better player than in 1982, when I had failed to qualify in my only other attempt. More importantly I was sober. I also reckoned that with Troon only a short drive from my home I would be going down every day anyway to watch so, this way, the worst that could happen was that I would get a competitor's pass allowing me free entry. As an Eisenhower Cup player I got an exemption from pre-qualifying and went straight into the final qualifying tournament. Only ten players out of 120 from each of the four qualifying courses were to go through to the Open, so it was a tall order. However, I was due to play at Irvine Bogside, which is a course I knew well and had scored low on before. I was drawn with a very good American professional, Tom Purtzer, who was easily one of the best players in the field. Playing with someone of his quality and professionalism obviously helped me, as I shot a 68 in the first round which placed me seventh overnight. I knew I had given myself a great chance to make the Open and had to make sure I made the most of my opportunity the next day.

If I was nervous at the start of the second round, the way I began soon put me at ease. I got off to a flying start. I birdied the first, a par four, then *eagled* the par five second and just knew it was going to be my day. A poor wedge onto the fourth green cost me a shot, but birdies at the sixth and eighth soon had me back on track. I parred the next three holes before picking up a bogey at the twelfth. I then worked out that if I parred the rest of the round it would be enough to get me in; so I just stayed calm and forced myself not to go for too much. The tactic worked a treat and I qualified comfortably in joint third place with two rounds of 68. I could hardly believe it. I had actually qualified for the Open, the greatest golf tournament in the world. It seemed impossible but I'd done it. The alcoholic who had been on the verge of suicide and banned from the game was going to be mixing, in a few days' time, with the very best golfers in the world. It was to be an incredible week.

GRAHAM RANKIN

European Tour star

Barclay and I must seem like the odd couple to a lot of people. He was the alcoholic who drank as much as he could get his hands on before venting his fury at anyone and everyone. I was the calm one who would sit chatting quietly in the corner over just one or two pints. I suppose it does seem odd in a way but Barclay has been one of my closest friends for more than ten years. We first got to know each other through the amateur golf ranks in the early 1980s and got on well together from the start.

In that time I have seen him behave in the worst ways imaginable. Some of the things he has said to people have been unforgivable. When he drank he really would become a monster to a lot of people and, not surprisingly, they would try to keep out of his way. Sober, he is one of the gentlest, most good-natured human beings you could ever hope to meet. Once he was drunk, however, he just became a completely different person. The way he would change left you wondering if it could really be the same person. Fortunately I knew how to handle him, and, if I sensed he was about to overstep the mark, I would grab him by the scruff of the neck and tell him in no uncertain terms it was time to leave. I was the only person who could handle him, and if he decided to have a go at me I would just let it go in one ear and out the other. I would just tell him it was time for him to go to bed and he would never normally argue. He knew that whenever I got a grip of him it was time to go. Maybe his subconscious would tell him that if I was stepping in then it was time to knock it on the head before he got himself into real trouble!

The next day would always start with a phone call from Barclay full of remorse and asking who he owed apologies to. I would fill him in on the night's events, telling him what he'd said and who he'd said it to. He would always be mortified and almost doubt that he could behave in such a way; then he would do the rounds saying sorry to those people he had offended. He knew the way he was behaving was wrong, but he didn't know what to do about it. He just couldn't help himself. He got on well with everybody he met when he was sober, but it's not surprising that he lost a lot of friends while he was drinking, because he did treat some of them appallingly. He was always a good friend to me if I needed help or advice about anything, though, and at that time, if you wanted to be Barclay's friend, you just had to take the rough with the smooth – or perhaps the Hyde with the Jekyll.

The saddest thing about the way Barclay drank in the 1980s is that, although he was still a very good player, he could have been a great player. If it hadn't been for the booze he would probably have made millions by now, but the drink was killing both him and his game. He has an unbelievable amount of talent; one of the most naturally gifted players I have ever seen in either the amateur or professional game. He had just about everything. He was a great driver off the tee as well as a fantastic irons player. He really could play every shot in the book. He was like a Trevino or Ballesteros the way he would conjure up shots that other players wouldn't even dream of attempting; but the booze stopped him from ever fulfilling his potential. I was on the course with him many times during tournaments when he was slugging back cans of lager on the way round. It was the only way he could settle down enough to play well. I believe that if his drinking had never reached that stage then he could have been one of the world's leading professionals, challenging for the majors and playing in the Ryder Cup instead of the Walker Cup. I think he realised this when he was banned for a year by Cochrane Castle, which turned out to be the best thing that ever happened to Barclay's game.

The ban made him face up to his drink problem and realise how he'd wasted a lot of his talent for so long. The way he played when he came back to golf proved that he was an even better player when he was sober, and I know he regrets the way he behaved in the earlier part of his career. He came back far more focused on his game and determined to be the best player he possibly could. If he'd had that attitude back in the early 1980s then there is no telling just how good he could have been. The good thing, however, is that Barclay doesn't dwell on yesterday, instead he just tries to make the most of today.

I remember the day he told me he had leukaemia. I was one of the first people he told and as soon as I picked up the telephone and heard his voice I knew there was something seriously wrong. There are not many people who could come through something like that, and he didn't kid himself or me about how serious it was. We both knew he could die, but Barclay has tremendous will-power and determination, and wanted to get better for his wife and daughter. In a strange way I think the alcoholism helped him. The way he tackled that showed him that he had the strength of character to take on a serious illness and gave him confidence that he could beat his cancer.

Barclay has been like a guiding light for me for many years and taught me to believe in myself. When we were amateurs together he was the one who gave me the confidence to believe I was good enough to turn professional and do myself justice in the pro game. Now I'm as desperate as he is to see him back at his best on the golf course. I know he wants to have a go on the Seniors Tour in a couple of years, and I'd love to see him having a crack at that because he could be one of the stars. Now he has beaten the cancer he just needs to rebuild his strength again, and I have no doubt that his game will still be in great shape. With his natural ability and determination to succeed he'll do really well on the Seniors Tour and I can't wait to see him out there playing at the top of his game again.

SEVEN

Open Glory

The Open. The biggest, the best, the most historic and, quite simply, the greatest event in golf. Anyone who has ever swung a club has, surely at one time or other, dreamed of sinking the winning putt on the eighteenth before lifting the famous Claret Jug. Never mind winning it, even making it on to the first tee is an unbelievable achievement. When you consider how many millions of people play golf around the world, it really is only a tiny, tiny percentage who are ever lucky enough to play in this wonderful championship. They really are the very best of the best. And, for four glorious days in July 1997, I was one of them. I didn't win the Open, but I played in it, made the cut and, for a short, magical time on the first day, led the field. It was an experience I will never, ever, forget.

The qualifying finished on Monday, 14 July, and I was up early the next day to head down to Royal Troon to register and play a practice round. The good thing about celebrating an achievement like qualifying for the Open when you are a recovering alcoholic, is that no drinking means no hangovers, so getting up early the next day is easy! I'm sure there were a few qualifiers that morning in a far more delicate state than me.

I picked my caddie and good friend, Ian McCosh, up at 6.30 a.m. to head down to Troon because I wanted to spend as much time as possible there soaking up the atmosphere – and it was amazing. Even at that time in the morning the whole place was buzzing. Royal Troon is an immaculate course in a beautiful part of Ayrshire and is a wonderful venue for the world's greatest golf tournament. When I got there I just looked at the huge spectator stands, the tented village, the practice and media facilities and had to pinch myself to make sure it was all real. Then I started to notice other players – some of the best golfers in the world – milling about, heading for the first tee or the practice area. To think that I was about to share the stage with them was an awesome feeling. I could barely believe it. My life just seemed to be getting better and better. I was the luckiest man on the planet. It wouldn't have surprised me if I'd won the jackpot on the lottery next, the way things were going.

Soon after arriving, Ian and I bumped into the captain of Royal Troon, Dave Smyth, who told us that Nick Faldo had been practising since 5.30 that morning! It seemed a bit extreme, but probably explains why he was the best player in the world for so long. I wanted an early practice round and Dave told us that Ignacio Garrido was the only name down for the 7.30 a.m. slot so I went along to ask if I could join him. When he failed to show I went ahead anyway on my own. I was quite happy to play a practice round by myself as I wanted to savour every moment of what was happening to me and didn't want to have to worry about chatting or being polite to someone else.

The whole experience seemed even more unreal when I saw who was going out in front of me. Only three of the biggest names in the sport: three times Open winner Nick Faldo, Lee Westwood and Andrew Coltart. I considered asking to join them as I knew Lee and Andy, but thought better of it. I reckoned I would be able to soak up more of the occasion if I stuck to my plan of going round alone. I didn't really keep my score on the way round and was just enjoying hitting the ball again on a course I knew pretty well, but it was still nerve-racking even if there were another two days to go until the competition started. Even for the practice rounds there were plenty of spectators dotted around the course who would cheer every shot I hit, followed up with shouts like: 'Get in there wee man.' What a feeling!

After lunch I went out to the practice ground, but ended up spending more time watching in awe than hitting balls. It was like a *Who's Who* of golf. The best – and richest – players in the world were all going about their business and I was right there among them. Bloody hell, I was one of them! My emotions kept switching between pride, wonder and sheer terror. But I told myself it didn't matter what happened on Thursday, I had already won my own, personal tournament just by qualifying so as long as I didn't embarrass myself by shooting 90 or missing a six inch putt on live television, I was quite happy to take whatever hand the golfing gods decided to deal me.

On Wednesday I headed down to Troon again for another round and some more practice. I was planning to make the most of every single second of an experience I knew I might never get the chance to enjoy again. This time I was a bit more sociable and played a fourball with three Scottish friends playing in the tournament: fellow amateur Craig Watson and professionals Raymond Russell and Dean Robertson. Craig and I challenged the pros and put our money where our mouths were with a small wager. Our confidence was obviously well-placed as we stole the match on the last green. I expect we'll get our money one day!

After lunch I hung around at the practice ground again and generally continued to enjoy the atmosphere. My caddie Ian McCosh was also with me and he was like the cat who got the cream. I almost had to physically drag him away at the end of the day, he was having such a great time seeing all these wonderful golfers close up. Even though they were among the biggest names in world sport, and most of them hadn't a clue who I was, they couldn't have been more pleasant. Everyone was tremendously polite and friendly, but late on Wednesday afternoon I suddenly realised that the serious business was only a few hours away. The star-gazing and daydreaming was great fun, but I knew if I didn't get back in touch with reality pretty quickly I could be brought down to earth with an almighty crash. Also, Ian would never forgive me if he was on worldwide television carrying the bag of the worst player in the tournament from one side of the fairway to the other. Driving home to Johnstone soon reminded me I led a slightly different kind of life to the likes of Tiger Woods, Nick Faldo and Ernie Els.

When the draw was made my friends Raymond Russell and Dean Robertson were convinced it was fixed. I was to play in a threeball for the first two days with two of the nicest men in world golf: England's Jim Payne and Peter O'Malley from Australia. Raymond and Dean told me I could not have asked for a better pair to go round with and they were right. Jim and Peter knew I would be nervous and put me completely at ease. They were friendly but also had the knack of knowing when to talk and when to keep quiet and they definitely helped me to relax.

I had hoped for an early tee off time on Thursday because I didn't want to have to hang about getting nervous, but my wish was not to be granted as the three of us were due off at 2.45 p.m. I got there in plenty of time and headed for the practice ground, but I was so nervous that I had to go to the toilet three times! The course was packed with thousands of spectators and there seemed to be television cameras everywhere I looked. Playing in the Open is a nerve-racking experience for the most experienced professionals in the world, so you can imagine what it was like for a mere amateur like myself. If it hadn't been for my past I would have been sorely tempted to knock back a shot of brandy just to steady my nerves!

As my start time approached, Ian and I headed over to the starter's tent and got ready. At a time like this you need your caddie to be a calming influence, but he was as nervous as me, and I had visions of him dropping the bag and spilling my clubs everywhere in front of millions of television viewers. Fortunately, when the crunch came, Ian discharged his duties as efficiently as ever, and certainly played a major part in what was to follow.

There were big stands at the back and side of the first tee and when the announcer called my name a huge cheer went up. I was shaking so much I must have resembled a jelly. Ian handed me my driver and I knew there was no turning back. Just teeing the ball up was an ordeal. My hand was trembling so much I could barely get the tee into the ground, never mind balance the ball on top of it. Once it was in place I just concentrated on going through my usual routine – and prayed to God I wouldn't shank it. At that moment in time I would have given every penny I owned for a guarantee that I would hit my drive cleanly. I took a few steps back, took a couple of practice swings, then stepped forward again and addressed the ball. There was a very strong wind at Troon that day, but luckily it was behind us on the front nine so I knew I didn't have to try to really belt the ball. I just wanted to make a nice, easy swing and knock it down the middle. Unfortunately, there is only so long you can stand still over the ball without moving before someone calls for medical attention, so there was nothing left to do but hit the shot. In the end it was not the best tee shot of my life, but it was certainly not my worst. I hit it reasonably well, albeit with a slight hook, and the ball flew off the tee and was picked up by the wind which, incredibly, carried it to about two yards from the front of the green. I had hit it far from perfectly, but if anyone had offered me that tee shot beforehand I would certainly have taken it.

I headed off down the fairway pretty pleased with my start to the Open and extremely relieved not to have done anything daft. The first hole at Troon is a 364-yard par four, and when I reached my ball I told myself to concentrate on just getting it into a reasonable position on the green to make par. But I hit a dream of a chip which ended up a foot from the hole to give me a simple tap-in and a birdie. There was a massive roar from the giant stand around the first green and suddenly I was in the tournament. That birdie settled me down and gave me the confidence to do my best and enjoy the day. Hopefully it also allayed my two professional playing partners' fears that they were in for a long day, continually waiting for me to find my ball in the rough.

If I had got off to a dream start, then things were about to become more unreal as I teed the ball up at the par four second. The wind was at my back, and before the day had started I'd planned to hit an iron off the tee because I was worried that my driver would carry the ball to the bunker which sits a long way up the fairway. However, after standing there looking down the fairway for a few moments I turned to Ian and said: 'I'm hitting the driver.' Ian looked at me curiously for a second, obviously wondering if all the excitement had gone to my head, before asking: 'What about the bunker?' But I brashly told him: 'I don't care about the bunker, I'm hitting the driver.' He handed me the club, obviously still concerned about my mental well-being, then stepped back. I teed the ball up, went through my usual routine, then *smack*. I absolutely smoked it. It was undoubtedly one of the best drives I have ever hit. The wind got hold of it and the ball went fully 400 yards, missing the bunker by inches. It ended up about five yards short of the green, but with a tricky pitch needed if I wanted to attack the hole. I was feeling brave and, buoyed by the confidence I'd gained already, I decided to gamble. To get near the hole I had to aim my pitch into the bump at the side of a bunker by the green. If I got it wrong the ball could either end up in the bunker or a long way past the hole. It was a risk, but a calculated one, and it paid off. The ball ended up about 10 to 12 feet from the hole, giving me a great opportunity for my second birdie in as many holes. Standing over the ball, my nerves had all but disappeared as I knew I was in great form. I also knew the ball was in the hole the second it left my putter and suddenly, just a few minutes after being a quivering wreck on the first tee and with a bladder I could barely control, I was two under after two holes and the crowd were going mad. A group of friends from Cochrane Castle were following me round and they were going absolutely wild. I don't think they could believe what was happening. I know how they felt.

At the par four third I decided it was time to calm down a bit and make sure I didn't get carried away. A burn was looming up ahead, running across the fairway, and I didn't want to blow my good start by going into it, so I decided to hit a long iron off the tee. This time there was no last-minute change of plan and I ended up in a reasonable position just short of the burn. I knocked a wedge on to the green before two putting for par and heading for the par five fourth where I knew a birdie was a possibility.

I reverted to my driver off the tee and hit it pretty cleanly up the middle, leaving me with a good chance of getting on the green in two. I took my three iron and hit a beauty, leaving me with a 25 foot eagle putt. I missed by a foot but rolled the next one in for my third birdie in four holes. It was a start I wouldn't have dared dream of, but it was real and it was happening. I had to keep telling myself to keep concentrating and play my natural game. I had seen in the morning that players were scoring well in the first nine before running into real trouble on the back nine because of the ferocious wind, so I knew there was a lot of hard work ahead. But despite my efforts to be calm, I couldn't help the buzz I was getting from the way I was playing. There were leaderboards all over the course, and to look up and see the name Howard up near the top at three under par after just four holes was amazing – and it was about to get better.

The fifth hole at Royal Troon is a longish par three, and I knew just avoiding a bogey would be a good result, so I was pretty relieved to see my five iron tee shot land on the green. I then took my regulation two putts and headed for the sixth pretty satisfied with my par.

The sixth is the longest hole on the course. A 577 yard par five but, with the wind behind me, I knew it was a birdie opportunity. I hit a good drive followed by a three wood which stopped on the green. I had given myself a great chance and I didn't waste it. Two putts later I had my birdie, was four under par and, incredibly, was joint leader. I couldn't believe what was happening. I expected to wake up at any moment and find the whole thing was a dream. Only I'd never had a dream that felt this good before.

The seventh was a par four and I hit my approach shot to 20 feet from the hole. Not ideal, but it gave me a chance to make par. My first putt wasn't great and left me with a six-footer. As any golfer knows these aren't easy at the best of times, never mind in front of a huge crowd and millions more watching at home. But my nerve held and I stroked the ball home to stay at the top of the leaderboard on four under.

Next came the eighth, the famous Postage Stamp hole. I hit a cracker of a seven iron off the tee, leaving myself with a four foot birdie putt to take the lead outright. I'd barely been able to take my eyes off the leaderboard the whole time and just kept staring at my name up there ahead of the best players in the world. Now here I was with the chance to lead the Open outright, something very few players experience in their lives. The putt was slightly tricky, downhill and downwind, and one I would usually expect to make under normal circumstances. But these were not normal circumstances. These were circumstances I had never encountered before and, to be brutally honest, I lost my nerve. I was just four feet from the hole but, as I stood over the putt, I was terrified I was going to knock it straight past, off the green and into a bunker. It wasn't just nerve-racking, it was absolutely terrifying. After what seemed to me like an eternity, but was actually just a few seconds, I drew my club back and hit the ball, dribbling it six inches past the hole. My chance had passed but at least I made my par, and I consoled myself with the thought that it could have been much, much worse. At least I hadn't become the first golfer in Open history to knock a four foot putt out of bounds which, at one stage, had felt like a real possibility.

There was only one more hole before the turn and the backward nine headfirst into gale-force winds. I was determined not to drop a shot at the par four ninth as I knew there were bogeys ahead. Fortunately, my plan worked and I made a pretty straightforward par; hitting a drive, iron into the green then two-putting. I'd reached the turn in a four under par 32, better than in my wildest dreams, and no matter what happened from then on I knew this was a day I would remember for a long, long time. I had played better than I could ever have hoped on the front nine and the strong wind at my back had certainly helped. Now I was about to find out just how good – or bad – I was by playing the back nine into a fierce headwind. Ian had assured me at the start of the day that, by the time I went out, the wind would have died down. It was about the only thing he got wrong all day.

I picked up my first bogey of the round at the par four tenth when my approach shot missed the green. However, in these conditions, a bogey was a decent score on some of these holes. And it certainly wasn't to be my last.

The eleventh is a fairly long par four and I simply could not reach the green in two. The wind was unbelievable and it was impossible to get any sort of distance on the ball at all. When I sunk my second putt I was again quietly satisfied I'd only dropped one shot as any one of these holes could prove disastrous in the conditions we were playing in. So, to pick up a birdie at the next hole was a very welcome bonus. It was a par four and I hit a decent drive followed by a nine iron on to the green. It left me about 18 feet from the hole; a difficult chance, but a chance nonetheless. I took my time over the putt and rolled it in for a birdie which settled me down again after the torrid time I'd had on the previous two holes.

The thirteenth is a very long par four, particularly in the wind we were up against. For the second hole in a row I was left with an 18 foot putt, only this time it was for a bogey, not a birdie. But I was just as pleased when I made it. This was another hole where just dropping one shot was a decent result, but it meant I was back to two under par.

In the atrocious conditions it was a relief to stand on the tee of the fourteenth because it's a par three. With distance no problem for the first time since the turn, I knew par was essential if I wanted to keep my great round going. Fortunately, I did just that. I didn't try anything too risky and just knocked my tee shot on to the green then two putted for par. There were only four holes to go now and I was desperate not to drop any more shots. To finish level under the circumstances would have been a great effort, but to end up two under par was better than I would ever have dared hope. Ian kept telling me: 'Keep going, keep going,' but I was sure something was bound to go wrong sooner or later. It all just seemed too good to be true. Ian's role that day cannot be overestimated. I was worried about making mistakes in the strong wind and was trying to be cautious in my club selection. But he kept advising me to take one club more and was right every time. His efforts were even more remarkable given the fact he could hardly see by the end of the round because his glasses were steaming up as he got more and more excited!

The fifteenth is a straightforward par four – when there is not a gale blowing across the course. However, I managed to negotiate my way up the fairway before two putting for a par. I was nearly home.

The sixteenth is probably the easiest of the three par fives on the course, but a birdie was a virtual impossibility in the wind. I hit my first two shots pretty well but was still left needing a three iron to reach the green with my third! Fortunately I hit it well before taking the regulation two putts. Another par. And another excellent return given the conditions, but I still had a lot of work to do before my day was over.

The seventeenth is a long par three, 223 yards, and I had real concerns about reaching the green with anything other than my driver. Eventually, I decided to go for my three wood and hit one of the best shots of my life. I caught it absolutely perfectly and left the ball on the edge of the green, about 25 feet from the hole. Afterwards, some of my Cochrane Castle mates who were following my round told me they reckoned it was my best shot of the day. I wouldn't argue. I two putted for a very welcome par and knew I just had to summon up one last effort.

On the eighteenth tee though, I had a problem. I knew the wind was too strong for me even to reach the fairway with my drive. But I also knew that even if I got a bogey five I would still finish the round under par and give myself a great chance of making the cut the next day. Sensibly, instead of going for broke I played safe and made sure of the five to come back in 38 for a one under par round of 70. It was good enough to end the day in joint sixth place and I could hardly believe what was happening as I signed my scorecard. I was level with Angel Cabrera, Davis Love III, Andrew Magee and Jesper Parnevik. One shot ahead of us were Greg Norman, Fred Couples and Justin Leonard, while Darren Clarke and Jim Furyk shared the lead after each shooting 67. Here I was, an amateur golfer from Johnstone who'd spent 20-odd years on the sauce, playing with – and beating – the best in the world. It was unbelievable.

Before heading home I had to go to the press tent, which was almost as exhausting an experience as the 18 holes I'd just played; but it was a great buzz having what seemed like every golf writer in the world wanting to quiz me about my round. I had never known anything like it and I was determined to enjoy every second.

Inevitably, journalists from the Scottish press were aware of my drinking history and it was an obvious topic for them to ask me about. I've always had a very good relationship with the press so I just decided the best thing for it was to be honest. The overseas journalists who had never even heard of me could probably not believe their ears when I started telling the stories about my drinking, and the next morning every paper in the country, and many throughout the world, knew about my past. The first four words of the *Daily Record*'s spread about me were: 'Reformed alcoholic Barclay Howard . . .' But I really didn't mind. I was proud of what I had achieved and just hoped that reading my story might help other people battling similar problems draw a bit of inspiration and realise that no matter how bad things look, there is a light at the end of the tunnel.

Gordon Simpson summed up my feelings perfectly in the *Record* when he wrote of my round: 'It was the stuff of fiction, but reality had been all too harsh for Howard in the past for him to worry too much.' I was completely candid when I described my past problems to the press lads that night. I said of my dark days just a few years earlier: 'If I drank one, I'd want to drink twenty. That was the problem in the old days. I would go out to play with six cans of lager in my golf bag. I had to, I couldn't play otherwise, because as I dehydrated I needed more alcohol to stop the muscles seizing up. Nowadays I can't play *with* a drink, which is great – I don't wake up every morning wondering who I've offended.' I went on: 'It took me until 1991 to realise I had a problem. Everybody else knew it in 1987. I was hurt about being banned from golf and decided to join Alcoholics Anonymous. Drink had turned me into an idiot.' Most people would probably not want to tell the newspapers that sort of thing about themselves but I saw no point in trying to hide my past. I was ashamed of the way I'd behaved in the past but I was also proud of the way I'd recovered and, like I said before, if it helped just one other alcoholic from giving up hope then it was worth having it splashed all over the newspapers. During the press conference I also took the chance to dedicate my opening round to my mum who was recovering in hospital from an operation at the time.

The golf writers lapped it all up, but treated me very fairly the next day, painting my battle with the booze in a sympathetic light and helping me to show what can be achieved once you admit to yourself you've got a problem and seek help.

I finally got home to Tish and Laura-Jane about 10.30 that night and should have been absolutely shattered, but I was far too excited to sleep. I wanted to relive every shot, every moment, over and over again in my mind's eye. Tish also wanted to know every single detail. She had not come down because she thought she would be too nervous, but she had watched on the television and was as delighted as I was that the day had gone well.

I got what sleep I could but was up early the next day because I'd agreed to do a live television interview with the BBC at 8.30 a.m. before my round an hour and 20 minutes later. I should have been shattered when I got there after everything that had happened the day before and my lack of sleep, but I was so excited by the whole thing that I was raring to go.

As I prepared for the second round I knew I had an excellent chance of making the cut and playing the last two rounds. Due to the weather, the scoring had been high the day before and I reckoned a 75 or better in the second round would be good enough. The wind had gone by now and I knew, if I kept my head and didn't try anything rash, there was definitely a chance.

Despite the improvement in the weather I found the second day tougher. I started well enough and at one stage was back to three under for the tournament, but although the magical touch I seemed to have acquired the previous day hadn't exactly disappeared, I wasn't able to produce quite the same form. I really had to dig in and in the end was pleased with my 74 – one better than my target. My prediction that it would be good enough to qualify proved to be accurate. While some of the best players in the world were on their way home early, I was going to be spending the weekend at Troon playing in the closing stages of the greatest golf tournament on the planet. I was the only non-professional to make the cut, guaranteeing me the coveted Silver Medal for best amateur – the first Scot to win it since the legendary Charlie Green in 1962.

After I had handed my scorecard in and done the press bit again I headed off to the practice ground to work on a couple of things I felt hadn't gone so well that day. While I was there Vijay Singh, one of the world's finest players, came up to me, shook my hand and congratulated me on winning the Silver Medal. It was a simple gesture, but that was the moment when it sank in what I'd achieved. I almost cried, but instead made do with giving Big Ian a hug. Goodness knows what anyone watching must have thought! Later on Ernie Els saw me walking on the other side of the road, so he crossed over so that he could shake hands with me and say: 'Well done.' It was another special moment for me in a very special week and I headed home to my wife and daughter a very proud man. When I got in and hugged Tish my emotions finally got the better of me and I have to admit I cried.

After everything I'd been through, all the bad years I'd had with the booze, I finally knew exactly what it was like to really be happy. I had my wonderful wife, my beautiful daughter and I was in the middle of the most amazing golfing experience imaginable. I was on an incredible high and, best of all, had not touched so much as a drop of alcohol to get me there.

I headed back to Troon on Saturday morning for the third round knowing I could just relax and enjoy myself. No matter what happened over the last two days, I would be finishing the tournament as top amateur and Silver Medal winner, and I would have shown the world how I could play. I was still keen to do well, though, and finish as high up the field as possible, so I was determined to keep on giving a good account of myself over the weekend.

An American, Jerry Kelly, was my playing partner on Saturday and for more than two thirds of the round things were going great. As I stood on the tee at the fifteenth I was one under for the round and looking in good shape to recover some of the shots I had lost on Friday. Then disaster struck. The fifteenth has got out of bounds down the right-hand side of the fairway and half of Ayrshire down the left. No prizes for guessing which way I sent the ball. As I said afterwards, for some reason I just decided to give it a whack. I ended up taking seven, a triple bogey, and was furious with myself for being so careless. But my troubles weren't over yet.

At the par three seventeenth I missed the green with my tee shot and ended up with a bad lie in the rough. I took a double bogey five. I followed this up with a bogey at the last to finish the round with a five over par 76. I was gutted. Up until the fifteenth I'd been playing well and thought I was in for my second sub-par round in three days. To finish five over from that position was a pretty poor performance and I was very disappointed. But at least I had a chance to make amends the next day in the final round when Tish and Laura-Jane would be coming to the course to support me for the first time in the tournament. I suspected it was going to be an emotional day and I wasn't wrong.

My disappointment at the way Saturday's round had ended was lifted when I picked up the next day's papers. Once again the press had been incredibly kind to me and it really was hard to read some of the stuff that was being written about me without bursting into tears. For a journalist like Hugh McIlvanney, one of the best-respected sports writers in Britain, to write more than 800 words on an amateur golfer must be just about unheard of. Even now, when I look back at what he wrote in the *Sunday Times*, I can feel the tears welling up. He referred to the 'towering figures' of the game who had not made the cut and said I was 'still there to live out the dreams of every club golfer in the land'. He added: 'And thousands of them on the course were determined to let him know how proudly they identified with an achievement that must rank as heroic.'

Fortunately, once I'd finished reading about my sudden celebrity status and got back to the business of playing golf, I did not pick up on Sunday where I'd left off on Saturday and I went round in a fairly satisfactory 72. I played with another American, Tommy Tolles, who turned out to be one of the game's true gentlemen. He was the perfect playing partner: friendly, charming and a very good golfer. In fact, he does so well on the US Tour that I had hardly slept the night before as I was so nervous about going round with someone of his calibre. We teed off earlier, at 9 a.m., but even at that time the weather was great. It was warm and sunny and that seemed to put everyone in a good mood. Tommy and I chatted all the way round and he even took the time to have a natter with Tish and Laura-Jane during the round. At the twelfth tee he spotted them in the crowd waving at me even though I had not noticed them. He pointed them out, saying: 'I think those two know you.'

The highlight of the day was coming up the last. We had both fired our second shots on to the green and I was determined to finish with a par on a hole I had struggled with throughout the championship. As we approached the green Tommy was about five or six yards ahead of me and the crowd were cheering us both. Suddenly, he stopped walking, turned to me and said: 'This is for you boy', and let me walk ahead. Well, the crowd just erupted. I have never heard a noise like it. Due to all the publicity I had received over the previous three days everyone knew my history and what I had been through. I felt about ten feet tall as I strode up that fairway and on to the green. The entire gallery was on its feet clapping and cheering. I had to fight hard not to burst into tears and it was a moment I'll remember for the rest of my life. As I got caught up in all the emotion of the occasion I almost forgot I had a round of golf to finish!

I had left myself with a 15 foot putt at the last for a birdie and a level par round. It really would have been the perfect end to an unbelievable week if I made it. As I lined up the putt I could sense the thousands of people in the crowd willing it to drop in. Then, as it was on its way, the screams of 'Get in the hole' rang out from all around. Sadly, the putt missed but I still made par – not a bad effort as I could barely see for the tears welling up in my eyes. When the ball went in there was another gigantic roar from the galleries. I swear it was as loud as I've heard for any putt to win the Open!

As I walked off the green Tish was in tears and I wasn't far behind. It seemed everyone wanted to congratulate me, shake my hand or pat me on the back. The feelings of personal pride and satisfaction were like nothing I had ever experienced before and I just didn't want the day to end.

The tears nearly flowed again a few hours later at the prize-giving. The Silver Medal is always awarded first at the Open and, if anything, the roar when my name was announced was even louder than when I'd sunk my putt on the eighteenth. Once more I found myself battling not to burst into tears. Justin Leonard had won the tournament and I couldn't believe it when he took the time to say a few kind words about me in his victory speech after being presented with the Claret Jug. He congratulated me on my success, which brought another cheer from the crowd, and warned that the American Walker Cup team could expect to have their hands full with me a few weeks later. They were wonderfully kind words from a deserving champion and genuinely warm-hearted man.

Afterwards I had to go through all the press interviews and some of the Americans journalists kept asking me if I would be having a pint or two to celebrate. For some reason they seemed to have trouble understanding that I was an alcoholic and, no, a pint or two was not really on the cards. When they asked me about my new-found fame and wondered what it would be like for me to be unable even to go for a meal without being recognised, I told them: 'It should be all right, you don't find too many autograph hunters in a chip shop!'

Eventually, though, everything has to end and my glorious Open was no exception. There's no question I felt a tinge of sadness as Tish, Laura-Jane and I headed back to Johnstone wondering if I would ever have such a wonderful experience again. We went to our local Indian restaurant that night with Ian McCosh to celebrate – although the £35 I'd won off the bookies by sticking a fiver on myself to make the cut was unlikely to make Justin Leonard green with envy as he pocketed his £250,000 winner's cheque. There was a lot of laughter as we relived the highlights of the week and I didn't want the night to end. It was hard to believe I had to be back at work the next day.

When I think back now over everything that happened during those magical four days it's still hard to believe that it wasn't all a dream. The first and last days in particular will stay with me for the rest of my life. Even now, several years later, I can still recall every detail as if it all happened last week. Even things that didn't go well, like the last few holes of my third round, were immensely enjoyable. I think if I had shot 100 that day I would still have walked off the eighteenth with a big smile on my face. The support I received from the crowd just got better and better as the tournament went on. At the start, I'm sure, most of the spectators at Troon had never heard of Barclay Howard; but that didn't stop them getting right behind me. Then, when all the publicity came out on the second day about my past problems with alcoholism, they just seemed to take me even more to heart. Every shot I played was greeted with a huge cheer and any bad ones were followed with shouts like: 'Stick in wee man', or 'Get in there wee man'. As for the reception I got walking up the eighteenth at the end of my last round . . . well, words don't describe how that felt. I was walking on air.

The whole experience gave me the belief that I was good enough to mix it with some of the best golfers in the world, although a bit more experience at that level would almost certainly have saved me a few shots on the third round. It left me desperate to experience that atmosphere once more and as I left Troon on Sunday night I was determined to be back at the Open the following year. After all, as my caddie Ian McCosh said, I would have to defend my Silver Medal. But 12 months later I was to spend the 1998 Open in a hospital bed, barely able to move and waiting to die.

IAN McCOSH

Open caddie

There were so many unforgettable moments during that incredible week in 1997 when Barclay Howard became one of the most famous golfers in the world: his name at the top of the leaderboard; his putt for the outright lead; the roar from the crowd going up the last; the congratulations from Ernie Els and Vijay Singh; winner Justin Leonard's kind words afterwards . . . the list is almost endless. But for me there was one incident which summed the whole tournament up brilliantly – and Barclay wasn't even there to witness it.

After the last round on the Sunday everyone was coming up to Barclay to congratulate him. It seemed like every single person on the course wanted to pat him on the back or shake his hand and say 'well done'. Somehow, though, he got through the scrum only to be pounced on by the press who wanted to know every detail of the last round.

While the attention was on him, Lady Angela Bonallack, whose husband, Sir Michael, was secretary of the R&A at the time, and one of the best-known and most important golf officials in the world, came up to me and said how proud they were of Barclay. She added that they had been on his side the whole way round and then looked me in the eye as she told me: 'This will always be remembered as Barclay's Open.' They were lovely, lovely words which, in my opinion, told the whole story of the championship. When golf fans think back to 1997 and the Open at Royal Troon they know Justin Leonard emerged as the champion; but for most of them Barclay's performance is the enduring memory. Even non-golf fans remember the great story of the man who led the tournament and then told the world's press he was a recovering alcoholic. Lady Angela's words still make me want to cry when I think of them now because she captured the mood of everybody perfectly. It really was Barclay's Open.

Right from the Tuesday morning's practice round I

knew Barclay was going to have a great week. He was hitting the ball well and feeling good, Troon is a course he likes and I just had a feeling it was all going to go right for him. I had no doubt that he would make the cut and knew he had a great chance of winning the Silver Medal. But not even I was expecting the start he got off to: birdies at the first two holes and suddenly his name was on the leaderboard. My wee pal, the man I was caddying for, and there was his name, up alongside some of the greatest players in the world. Then it got better. When he was two under he asked one of the Cochrane Castle members watching him to take a picture of the leaderboard, but he refused, saying he'd only do it when Barclay was leading the field. I'm sure he was only joking, but he didn't have long to wait. When he birdied the sixth hole to go four under and share the lead it really did seem like a dream. Everything was going so well it just seemed too good to be true. Then came *that* putt on the eighth. I know Barclay says that the pressure of a chance to take the lead outright was just too much for him and that was the reason he dribbled it. However, I think the pressure built up because of the length of time he had to wait to hit the shot. His tee shot was a beauty and if he had just been able to walk up to the green and take his putt I have no doubt that he would have made it. Unfortunately, however, his two playing partners that day, Jim Payne and Peter O'Malley, both found bunkers by the green with their tee shots, and Barclay was left with a long wait before he was able to take his putt. It just gave him too much time to think about what he was about to do, otherwise I've no doubt he would have made it. Obviously the back nine were extremely tough that day because of the ferocious wind, so for Barclay to finish his round one under par was a fantastic achievement. Out of the best 150 or so golfers in the world taking part that day only a small handful broke par and Barclay was one of them. He deserved all the attention he got afterwards. The only disappointing thing for me was all the questions he faced about his past. Barclay has always been completely open about his alcoholism, but in a way, the grilling he got about his drinking took a slight gloss off the occasion for me. I thought the press should have concentrated on what a great round he'd had, but I suppose, in their eyes, the drinking was the story.

There was also a moment on the second day which I will remember forever. We went to the practice ground before Barclay's round. He stood hitting balls in a line with Davis Love III, Phil Mickelson, Fred Couples, Bernhard Langer and Seve Ballesteros and I remember getting very emotional as I thought: 'This is where Barclay should be, this is where he belongs.' Over the years I had seen Barclay play some wonderful, wonderful golf and he could easily have been as good as those guys, but his game was hampered by his lifestyle.

I am a few years older than Barclay but have known him since he was a small boy trying to make contact with the ball as he swung wildly with his left-handed clubs. In fact I first caddied for him as far back as 1969. As a result I've seen him at his best and his worst. And there is no doubt that his worst moments were bad. When Barclay took a drink he would turn into a nasty, nasty drunk. Some people get violent when they're drunk, some become friendly and want to cuddle you, some pass out and some, like Barclay, get very rude and obnoxious. He would become very aggressive and say things that were simply unacceptable. When he was sober he was a fantastic guy and a real pleasure to play a round of golf with. If he was playing in a medal competition at Cochrane Castle he would quite happily go round with high handicap players – something which some players of his standard just refuse to do. He wouldn't mind playing with them and chatting away to them and they'd think he was one of the nicest people they'd ever met. Later on in the clubhouse, however, once he'd had a good drink, he would turn into this completely unrecognisable person. He was protected to a fair degree at Cochrane Castle because he was such a good player and people knew what he was like when he was sober, but eventually he went too far and paid the price. In the long run it was probably a good thing he did, because once he stopped drinking his golf just got better and better; and it was pretty good to start with. He was an amazing character in the 1980s because there would be some Friday nights where I would have to take him home and help him into bed because he was so drunk. Then the next day he would get up and shoot two sub-par rounds to win a big tournament. I really have no idea how he did it but I'm glad he's stopped it now. If he hadn't then that week at Royal Troon would probably never have happened and Lady Angela Bonallack would never have said those words: 'This will always be remembered as Barclay's Open.' They were the loveliest words anyone has ever said about my great wee pal and I will take them to my grave.

EIGHT

What's Wrong With Me?

I was on a complete high for days after the Open ended. The media attention continued, and my friends and family were also delighted for me. People I had never even set eyes on before were coming up to me in the street to say well done. I honestly don't think I could have felt any prouder if I had won the tournament itself. I felt as if I was walking on air and the problems I had come through a few years earlier only served to increase my pride. I know Tish was also delighted for me and it was also an exciting time for Laura-Jane even though she didn't really know why. I was on top of the world and it felt good.

I received letters and cards from all over the world. One was from a retired army colonel who was living in Germany. Troon was the first time he'd ever been to the Open and on the first day he had been following the big names round like Tiger Woods, Colin Montgomerie and Nick Faldo when he saw my name on the leaderboard with the A for amateur after it. His letter said: 'From then on I became part of Howard's Army. I watched you all the way round on Friday, Saturday and Sunday.' It was incredible that someone would travel all that way and then spend his time watching a middle-aged, recovering alcoholic rather than the biggest names in the game. I was flattered and delighted I had been able to give him such an enjoyable holiday.

I also got a lot of letters from AA members saying what an inspiration I had been to them over the four days, which was very touching. I just hoped I was able to help some of them by showing that admitting you are an alcoholic does not mean that you have to give up on life or stop chasing your dreams. On the contrary, it had given me a new, better life and I was making the most of my second chance.

Robert Philip wrote in the *Daily Telegraph* a few days after the Open: 'Perhaps it is because so many of us can see ourselves in Barclay Howard that he touched the soul of the nation at Troon.' In the same interview I told him: 'I think there's a lot of people out there with the same unfortunate disease who were cheering me on, or maybe they knew someone who has it and I gave them hope that you can battle back from the brink of disaster.'

But it wasn't the praise and media attention that I liked. Admittedly it was nice to read some of the stuff that was being written about me, but as far as the adulation and hero worship went, I could really take it or leave it. What gave me the greatest pleasure was proving to myself what I was capable of. Even if nobody ever mentioned the 1997 Open to me again I don't think it would have made the slightest bit of difference. Nothing could take away the enormous satisfaction I felt at what I'd achieved. Even if I had let it all go to my head, I was about to be brought back down to earth with an almighty bump.

In early August I left for America with nine of my Great

Britain and Ireland team-mates determined to retain the Walker Cup which we had won so memorably two years earlier at Royal Porthcawl. After the way I had been playing for the previous two seasons, including at the Open just a couple of weeks earlier, I was confident of playing a major a part in what I hoped would be a famous victory. Sadly I couldn't have been more wrong – on both counts.

The other players under Clive Brown's captaincy were fellow Scots Graham Rankin, known as 'The Animal' because of his more than passing resemblance to the Muppets character of the same name; Craig Watson, Mike Brooks and Steven Young, along with Richard Coughlan, Keith Nolan, David Park, Gary Wolstenholme; and a very promising young player who was to cause quite a stir of his own at the Open the following year – 17-year-old Justin Rose. It was a good team and, while everyone knew that beating the Americans on their own patch would require a superhuman effort, we all believed we were capable.

Apart from a burning desire to spank the Yanks once more, I had another reason for wanting to do well. I chose one of the practice days to announce my retirement from international golf. I would play in the Walker Cup, represent Scotland in the Home Internationals the following month, then that would be it. I had been considering it for about two years, realising that, while representing Scotland and Great Britain in various competitions over the years had been a wonderful experience and given me countless fantastic memories, I had been missing out on important moments with my family. Being in America for the Walker Cup meant missing Laura-Jane's fifth birthday and her first day at school; important milestones that fathers should be part of. The clinching factor came while we were in New York before the match started and my mother-in-law sent a fax of one of Laura-Jane's drawings with a good luck message. I got a bit emotional at what I was missing back home. I was also beginning to resent the time I was having to spend practising my golf, instead of enjoying it as I had previously. To stay at the top, even in the amateur game, takes a tremendous amount of dedication and hard work. I used to get up at five o'clock in the morning to practice and I really didn't want to do that any more. I intended to keep playing tournaments around Scotland and had one eye on the professional Seniors Tour when I turned 50 in 2003, but for those reasons I'd had enough of playing at the top level of the amateur game. As I said at the time: 'This year has been perfect. I won my national title, I was lucky enough to get the Silver Medal at Troon and now I'm playing in the Walker Cup again. I want to go out on a high and you can't top this.'

The high I intended to go out on didn't just involve playing the Americans over the demanding Quaker Ridge course in New York however, it meant beating them. Victory over the USA on their own home ground would have been one of the greatest highlights of my career – even up there with winning the Silver Medal at Troon.

Our team probably wasn't as strong as the triumphant one from Royal Porthcawl, but it was pretty good nonetheless, with an ideal blend of youth and experience. Most of the boys had enjoyed a pretty good season and we were all in a very positive mood. We were definitely ready for the battle that lay ahead. Nobody was under any illusions about how tough it would be, but we all genuinely believed we had a good chance of retaining the trophy we'd won so memorably two years before.

Before the match started my team-mate Mike Brooks told the press I was the best amateur in the world and that I would lead us to a glorious victory. As a result of the way I was playing that season he said: 'There's nobody in the world to touch

Barclay in this form. He showed at Troon that he's the No.1 in the amateur game – either in Europe or America – and what he did in the Open gave the whole team an incredible lift. He's given us all the belief that we can beat the Americans in their own backyard. This course suits him perfectly. He nails the ball off the tee and his irons are just awesome.' As if this glowing tribute wasn't enough, Mike went on: 'I honestly don't think there is one member of the American team who fancies coming up against him. He's worth a point of a start to us. One man can't win the Walker Cup on his own but what Barclay does can go a long way to helping us retain the cup.' Kind words, but I'm sure by the end of the match Mike was wishing he'd never said them. I know I was!

My Open exploits had gained a lot of press coverage in America and I was probably the best-known European team member among the public over there. Even the Walker Cup press officer referred to it when he said: 'Barclay is a person who has overcome adversity and everyone out here loves him for that.'

Our captain Clive Brown was also generous in his praise beforehand, saying: 'Ever since we arrived in America people have been saying that we have the stars this time. They don't have Tiger Woods and we have Barclay. Every time his name crops up here it raises the profile of the Walker Cup and that can only be good. His Open display is hopefully a good omen. Two years ago Gordon Sherry captured the headlines at the Open and went on to inspire us to victory at Royal Porthcawl. Now I hope Barclay can do the same.' My hopes were the same as Clive's. Sadly, we were both well off the mark.

Nothing in our preparation was left to chance. We flew out a week early to make sure there would be no jet lag and to acclimatise ourselves to the 90 degree heat expected for the match. We were all put on a strict diet made up predominantly of pasta and rice to help keep our energy levels up in the intense heat. Even our clothing for the match was specially made to allow us to feel as comfortable as possible in the humidity. We were also convinced that Richard Coughlan's hole-in-one in practice at the 244 yard thirteenth would be an omen that we were in for a successful weekend. That illusion was to be quickly shattered.

The first morning was nothing short of a disaster for us as we were trounced 4–0 in the foursomes. One newspaper described our performance as 'a comedy of errors', another said we were 'pitiful'. Both descriptions were pretty accurate and I more than deserved my share of the blame. Clive paired me with Steve Young, a 20-year-old Walker Cup rookie, which was a sensible decision as we had played well together before for Scotland. Sadly we were soundly beaten 4 and 3 by Brad Elder and Joel Kribel. Steve hadn't been at his best but had played reasonably well. I, on the other hand, was awful. If someone told me beforehand I could play as badly as that in the Walker Cup I would have laughed in their face. I just couldn't believe how poor my performance was. Surely I couldn't play like that again, I thought; and I was right. I got worse.

Mike Brooks and Justin Rose went down 5 and 4 to Jerry Courville and Buddy Marucci. Poor Justin, who must have been incredibly nervous as it was, got off to the worst possible start by driving his tee shot at the first out of bounds. Mike then hooked the second ball into trees and Justin hit a tree with the next shot. By the time they lost on the fourteenth green, they were nine over par. Steven and I fared only marginally better. We were one down after eight holes, but then lost the ninth and tenth and never recovered. We were supposed to be the top two pairs, yet we managed just two birdies between us; nowhere near good enough to challenge our American opponents.

It looked like Great Britain and Ireland would get back on track in the third foursome when Gary Wolstenholme – who had been one of the heroes two years earlier at Royal Porthcawl when he beat Tiger Woods in the singles – and Keith Nolan won the first two holes against Jason Gore and John Harris. They then proceeded to lose seven out of the next nine, however, and their promising start turned into the heaviest defeat of the morning: 6 and 4. Only Richard Coughlan and David Park managed to put up any sort of a fight. Two down with three to play, they won the sixteenth, tied the seventeenth and then Richard had a six foot birdie putt at the last to claim a half point. But he missed, giving the USA their best start to the competition in 10 years. As we trooped into the clubhouse for lunch, skipper Clive Brown was a master of understatement when he said that we had 'made a lot of silly mistakes'.

Fortunately, things improved for the Great Britain and Ireland team in the afternoon singles. Unfortunately, things went from bad to worse for me. I was on the receiving end of another hiding from Brad Elder, one of my conquerors in the foursomes. He beat me 5 and 4 and I finished the day feeling absolutely gutted. This match was supposed to be the crowning moment of my wonderful season – of my whole career – and here I was being thrashed and playing like a Sunday afternoon hacker. I knew I wasn't right physically. I felt tired and weak but put it down to the heat. I certainly didn't think there was anything seriously enough wrong with me to cause the sudden slump in form I was suffering.

In the other singles matches, Steven Young and Craig Watson got us off to a great start by winning the first two ties out. Craig's culminated in a nail-biting finish after he earlier appeared to be cruisng to victory. He was three up with three to play against Steve Scott but then lost the sixteenth and

141

seventeenth. Craig then managed a par at the last but Scott had a 20 foot birdie putt to cap what would have been a remarkable comeback; winning the hole and halving the match. Luckily, he missed. A stream of birdies helped Steven Young to a 5 and 4 win over Duke Delcher. My foursomes partner had obviously found some form now he didn't have me to hold him back!

Justin Rose showed a great deal of character to win his match after the disastrous start to his Walker Cup career in the morning, but it looked like he was in for another difficult round when he three putted from four feet at the first. He drew level by winning the sixth with a bogey before taking the tenth and fifteenth with pars to set up our third win out of the top four singles. If we thought the tide had turned, however, we were mistaken. Randy Leen took charge in the back nine against Keith Nolan to record a 3 and 2 win. Jason Gore then beat Graham Rankin by the same score in the sixth singles to stretch the Americans' lead.

The last two singles were crackers, both going to the last hole. Richard Coughlan held his nerve superbly to birdie the eighteenth and grab a half point against Chris Wollmann, but sadly Gary Wolstenholme, who had gone up the last all square with John Harris, three putted to give America another valuable point. It all meant we ended the day trailing by eight and a half points to three and a half. The task we faced the next day if we wanted to hang on to the Walker Cup wasn't impossible, but it wasn't far from it. If things had been any worse they would have been calling it the Walkover Cup, as the Americans used to do when they dominated the competition in its early days.

I was very down that night. I'd played like I had never picked up a golf club before and really felt as though I'd let the rest of the boys down badly. I was probably the best amateur in Britain that year and yet I'd been hammered twice – and deservedly so.

I also felt dreadful physically. I was sweating heavily and felt exhausted. I knew there was no way I should play the next day and went to tell Clive my decision. I was so distraught by what had happened I practically begged him not to play me. He just looked at me and asked: 'Do you want to play foursomes or singles?' I wondered if he'd heard me alright so tried again. 'Clive,' I said, 'I'm playing rotten and I'm not feeling well. There's no way I can play tomorrow, I'll just let everyone down again.' But he told me he wanted me to play and asked again if I'd rather play foursomes or singles. I chose the foursomes for the simple reason I would only have to hit half the shots so that would at least slightly limit the damage I could do.

The next morning we woke up in determined mood. All the boys knew we had a mountain to climb but there was no way we were going down without a fight. I was as ready as anyone and, despite still feeling well below my best, I was convinced I would make amends for my awful performance the previous day. Clive gave us a morning pep talk and told us that every match – every shot – that day counted and that, no matter what happened, we were in with a chance until the Americans reached that magical 12 and a half point mark. Sadly, despite our positive attitude, it didn't take them long to get there.

Clive changed the pairings around for the second day foursomes and put me with my great friend Graham Rankin. We went out against Buddy Marucci and Jerry Courville Jr, determined to grab a vital point for our side. I was desperate to play better because I knew I had performed well below my best the previous day. I was almost embarrassed by how I'd played and really wanted to make up for it; both because I felt I'd let my team-mates down and for personal pride. Unfortunately, it wasn't long before Graham and I were back in the clubhouse after being on the wrong end of a 5 and 4 thrashing. Once again

I had played embarrassingly badly and I really felt sorry for Graham. I knew I had let him, and the other boys, down, but just did not know what to do to get my game back together. Nothing was working right. I was missing the fairways by miles, my irons were dreadful and most of my approaches would be lucky to get anywhere near the greens. Even when we got on the putting surface I was just as bad. It was another humiliating and hugely depressing experience.

Two of our other pairs faired only marginally better. Steve Young and Craig Watson went down 3 and 2 to John Harris and Brad Elder, while Richard Coughlan and David Park lost by one hole to Duke Delcher and Steve Scott. That left the Americans needing just one more point for victory and if it hadn't been for a brave showing by Justin Rose and Gary Wolstenholme the whole thing would have been over by lunch. They had been one down after eleven against Randy Leen and Chris Wollmann but battled back to take the tie 2 and 1 to leave us trailing 11–4 going into the afternoon singles. Lunch was a pretty depressing meal for the second day running as, realistically, we all knew the match was pretty much over.

It was also completely over for me. I decided after my performance in the foursomes that there was no way I should play in the singles. If my form had improved and we had won then I would probably have changed my mind about not playing in the afternoon. As things were I went to Clive and made sure he was still planning to leave me out for the final round of singles. I was absolutely devastated by the way I had been playing and couldn't believe the slump I was in after the form I had shown all year. I also still felt awful and had experienced real problems dealing with the heat and humidity through the practice and match rounds. My personal disappointment was huge, but the worst part was feeling that I had let the rest of the boys down badly. I felt it was best for the team if I didn't play in the singles. The last thing they needed was someone who couldn't even hit the ball straight. I had gone over there as just about the biggest name in world amateur golf because of my exploits at Troon, and then I had played like a beginner. I just couldn't face another round. Clive was very sympathetic and understood totally. Mind you, after three thrashings he was probably glad of an excuse to get rid of me!

The final point the Americans needed did not take long to come. John Harris dealt the killer blow when he holed from three feet at the thirteenth to give him a resounding 6 and 5 win over Mike Brooks. It was fitting, really, as he had probably been the outstanding player from both sides over the weekend. It was also his sixth win out of six Walker Cup singles matches. A phenomenal record. Great Britain and Ireland did manage to pick up another 1½ points but it was scant consolation. Our sole win was recorded by debut boy Steve Young, who also won his singles the previous day, with a 2 and 1 victory over Joel Kribel. Our final half point came courtesy of Craig Watson who won the last hole to tie with Jason Gore. The other five singles matches were all lost.

Justin Rose put up a brave fight after a nightmare start. He was trailing Jerry Courville Jr by five holes at the turn but battled back before going down 3 and 2. But he did enough over the weekend to convince me and a lot of others that he has got a very big future in the game. He turned professional shortly after the following year's Open where he played so splendidly and, admittedly, it was probably a little too soon, but the pressure on him to do it was huge. He quickly found out how tough professional golf can be as he struggled badly in the first few months, missing the cut in each of his first 21 tournaments. I am delighted that he's doing better now and seems to have turned the corner. He's a great lad who has a tremendous appetite for golf along with a very good attitude to the game. After spending time practising with him prior to the Walker Cup and watching him close up under pressure, I have no doubt that he will make a big impact on the professional game.

In the other singles match David Park was convincingly beaten 4 and 3 by Buddy Marucci while Keith Nolan, Gary Wolstenholme and Richard Coughlan each lost 2 and 1 to Brad Elder, Duke Delcher and Steve Scott respectively. It gave the match a final score of USA 18 Great Britain 6 and, as I said, was undoubtedly one of the lowest points of my golfing career.

My disappointment was doubled by my poor personal performance. John Hopkins wrote in *The Times* after the match: 'All in all it was a very disappointing performance by a team widely believed to be the best prepared to leave these shores. One player after another failed to reproduce the form that they had shown at home – none more so than Barclay Howard, arguably the best amateur in the four home countries, who played three times and lost convincingly each time.' I couldn't have summed it up any better. I knew I had let the side down badly and what hurt most was not even being able to turn the match into any sort of contest. The result also reopened the debate about changing the match into America versus Europe, as had happened with the Ryder Cup some years earlier. It was an argument we hoped we had ended two years before at Royal Porthcawl and, I'm glad to say, quashed again at Nairn in 1999. It would be a tragedy if the Walker Cup became a Europe v USA contest. It might make sense in the professional game where everyone knows the top European players, but I doubt if the average British golf fan could name any of the top amateurs on the continent. It would lose a lot of the magic and not be as interesting for spectators.

On the last night at Quaker Ridge there was a reception and

meal for the players. Many of the American and British golfers had seen me tearing into the free booze at the post-match meal in 1995 and they expected the same sort of performance from me here. Luckily, although I'd ended up in quite a state at Royal Porthcawl, I had managed to behave myself and avoided offending anyone. I wasn't going to take that chance here. I sat with Tish and Graham Rankin at the meal and drank two bottles of beer. They tasted awful. I realised I just didn't want to drink and was doing so because I felt I should. When I finished the second bottle I just stood up and announced: 'That's it, I'm off to bed.' Drinking, and being around other people who were drinking, just wasn't what I wanted to do anymore. That Sunday night at Quaker Ridge was the last time I touched a drop of alcohol.

I have played in two Walker Cups and they have given me the greatest and worst moments of my golfing career. The win in 1995 was like no other feeling I have ever had from the game – even better than the Open at Troon. We had an outstanding team which performed exceptionally well. The elation I felt when we won is indescribable. It was a wonderful, wonderful moment. But there is no question that the 1997 Walker Cup at Quaker Ridge, New York, was far and away the lowest point of my career. I was absolutely gutted; not just with the hammering we received, but also with the way I'd performed. It was undoubtedly the worst I have ever played in a major competition and it still hurts me to think back to it. Things were so bad over the weekend that I even phoned home twice to ask my coach John Mulgrew if he had any cure from thousands of miles away. I told him I couldn't do anything right. He had a few suggestions but nothing seemed to work. I was not just having trouble with one aspect of my game, like failing to sink six foot putts or struggling to hit the fairway off the tee; it was everything. Nothing was working. It was like I had suddenly become a terrible player overnight and the harder I tried the worse I got. I also felt physically exhausted. I had expected the heat and humidity to take their toll, but I was surprised by how bad I felt. Of course, I didn't know at the time that I was already suffering from leukaemia. I certainly wasn't alone in the team in the way I under-performed, but I would be the first to admit I was the worst of the lot.

It is difficult to pinpoint precisely what was to blame for our dismal showing, but I believe that our plan to arrive a week early to become acclimatised backfired. It was a great idea in principle: to have a few days together as a team playing golf and getting used to the extremely hot and humid conditions. But I would say a lot of the problems we encountered once the match got underway were a result of playing too much golf in the week leading up to it. Everyone was physically drained by the time the competition got underway. Even the younger lads like Steve Young and Justin Rose were finding it hard going. We were a different team than the one which had won at Royal Porthcawl two years earlier. While still full of good golfers, the side at Quaker Ridge was not as strong and required more astute captaincy. Clive Brown is a great person but I do believe he handled the preparation for the competition wrongly. Before heading to New York we spent five days in Baltimore as guests of the Caves Valley Golf Club. It was a fantastic course with wonderful facilities and we were made to feel very welcome. That didn't mean we had to play golf at every opportunity, yet that's what we seemed to be doing. The preparation before Royal Porthcawl was spot on, but America was a different matter altogether. The heat alone made it physically draining to play as much as we did in the run-up to the start of the competition.

Every day we left the hotel early for breakfast at the club. We would then play a round in the morning before having lunch in the clubhouse. Afterwards we would be back out practising our driving, chipping, irons, putting, bunker play and every other shot imaginable before heading back to the hotel for dinner. But once we got there we would all go to our rooms for dinner instead of having a get together and group meal in the dining room. The only time we all had dinner together that week was on the night we arrived. After that it was room service every night, meaning that we missed out on valuable team bonding opportunities.

Although golf is basically an individual sport, there is no question that when it is played in a team format like the Walker Cup or Ryder Cup, a good team spirit is essential. When you get the mood right within the camp it really does make a difference to the way everyone feels and plays. If everyone is happy and enjoying themselves they are going to be more relaxed and better able to produce their best golf. If that team spirit is missing then the players are more likely to become insular and get uptight about things.

All the practice in the 90 degree heat was leaving us exhausted. Even the young lads like Justin were dripping in sweat by the end of the first hole each day, so you can imagine what it was like for an out of condition veteran like myself. It also meant that by the time the competition got underway we were all a bit stale from too much golf as well as feeling worn out by the heat. I believe a more gradual build up would have been of greater benefit so that we were ready to peak on the first day of the match, rather than have everyone turn up on the first tee slightly jaded. I, and some of the other players, felt at the time we were being asked to play too much in the run-up to the match but, in fairness to Clive, no one actually raised it with him and, as one of the senior players, I have to accept that was something I should have done. Obviously it was not Clive's fault that things went so disastrously wrong in the match, but a gentler week beforehand with slightly less golf would definitely have left us fresher once battle commenced.

All the Great Britain and Ireland boys had been due to go on from Quaker Ridge to the US Amateur Championship at Cog Hill, near Chicago, the following week. I had also intended to go but was having second thoughts because of my wretched form. Although Tish had flown out to Quaker Ridge, she would not be going on to Cog Hill and I was also missing Laura-Jane and wanted to get home. On top of that I was not feeling at all well, but I knew I would probably never get another chance to compete in the US Amateur Championship so, after a couple of days' hard-thinking, I decided to stay and play. After all, I didn't think I could get any worse!

My performance in the Walker Cup may not have been particularly memorable, but I was hailed as a hero shortly afterwards. When I got to Cog Hill I started to find a bit of form and was playing much better. In fact, I was the only member of the Great Britain and Ireland side to come through the two round qualifying tournament to claim a place in the matchplay stage of what is one of the biggest amateur golf tournaments in the world. It is a tough course but I shot a first-round 70 followed by a 71 the next day – comfortably good enough to qualify. At the end of the second qualifying round I had signed my card, handed it in and was relaxing in the clubhouse pleased to have come through, though disappointed that none of my Walker Cup team-mates had made it. My caddie, a teenage girl who was a member of the club, came in and asked me to autograph my ball for her so I dug it out of my pocket – and nearly had a heart attack. It was a Balata – not the type of ball I'd started out with. I had played the first 35 holes with a Pro-

90 but when I'd reached into my bag on the eighteenth tee I'd inadvertently pulled out the Balata and used it at the last hole without informing my playing partners of my change of ball which was a breach of the rules. It might seem like a minor oversight to non-golfers and one of those rules which gives golf its rather stuffy image in some quarters, but it was a huge blunder and I knew what the consequences would be – disqualification.

I stood staring at the ball for ages thinking I was seeing things. I thought that if I kept looking then I would realise I was mistaken and it didn't really have the word Balata stamped on it. I tried looking away, as if it would magically have turned into a Pro-90 when I looked back. Not surprisingly neither of these ploys worked and it didn't take long for the horrible realisation to dawn on me that I was well and truly shafted. Even if I had discovered the mistake before signing and handing in my score card just 30 minutes earlier I would have got off with a two-shot penalty. It was too late even for that now and I knew what I had to do.

I would, in all probability, have got away with it if I'd kept my mouth shut. If I had just popped the ball back in my pocket there is no way anyone would ever have known I had broken the rules. I could have gone out the next day and played in the matchplay competition without anyone being any the wiser. The only problem was that one person would have known – me. And there was no way I was able to do that. I love the game of golf too much to even think about cheating. So I walked in a daze towards the referee's office to confess my sin. When I got there I don't think the tournament officials could quite believe what they were being told. They knew I could have got away with it without being caught and must have thought I was mad or, if they knew about my past, that I had decided to celebrate qualifying by going back on the booze *big* time. But once they realised I was sane and sober they had no choice but to disqualify me. I was gutted. Why hadn't I ignored my little oversight? After all, it's not as if it made any difference to the outcome of my round. Frankly, I couldn't ignore it. I had broken the rules, albeit unwittingly and to no particular advantage, and I deserved to be disqualified. No matter how small the infringement was I would not have been able to live with myself if I'd kept quiet and carried on playing. I would have gone to my grave with a huge guilty secret hanging over me if I had gone on to win the tournament knowing that I had broken the rules. Anyway, with that sort of thing weighing on my conscience I would have been lucky to get the ball off the tee in the next round, so in a way I did myself a favour by not embarrassing myself the next day. Also, I had praise heaped upon me in America for what I'd done. The *Chicago Tribune* even carried half a page on the story calling me a 'Scottish hero' for owning up. I'm not quite a match for William Wallace but looking back I suppose it was nice to have such kind words written about me. 'Bloody idiot' might be the way some people might describe me for what I did. I certainly felt like one!

The whole episode was also sad for me because, finally, I was starting to play really well again. I had taken a few days' rest between the Walker Cup and the US Amateur to recharge my batteries and it had done me the world of good. When I arrived at Cog Hill I played just nine holes the day before the tournament started and decided that was enough practice. I knew I was hitting the ball much better and, although still feeling a bit tired, believed I was now playing well enough to have a chance of winning. I wasn't wrong. I shot 141 for the two qualifying rounds, easily beating the cut-off mark of 146 to get into the matchplay stage. Even if I had spotted my ball mix-up before handing my scorecard in and been given a two-shot penalty I would still have comfortably made it. It just wasn't meant to be, I guess, and anyway, I was desperate to get back to Tish and Laura-Jane after being away for so long. I planned to go home, have a couple of days' rest before getting in a bit of practice before preparing to represent Scotland in the Home Internationals – the tournament which I intended to be my last event at that level. It wasn't to work out that way and I never got my chance to have an international swansong.

Part of my preparation for the Home Internationals involved playing in the 36-hole Viking-Krus tournament at the Largs-Kelburne course in Ayrshire. As I headed for the course I tried to put the disappointment of the Walker Cup behind me and concentrate on regaining the form I had shown in the US Amateur. I want to win every tournament I play in, but with the Home Internationals just around the corner it was especially important for me to do well so I could head off to represent my country feeling good about myself and my game. As things turned out, I never even made it to the Home Internationals.

The first hole of the Largs-Kelburne course is a par three up a very steep hill. I took my seven iron out of my bag, knocked it up the hill and headed off to see how close I was to the pin. There was only one problem – I couldn't make it up the hill. I thought I was going to collapse as I tried to make it up what is no more than about a 160 foot climb. After just a few yards I was exhausted, out of breath, sweating buckets and had a terrible pain in my chest. I knew there was something seriously wrong, I just didn't know what. I even thought I might be having a heart attack. In the end I had to hitch a lift in someone's buggy to make it to the top.

After the first, the next 16 holes at Largs-Kelburne are pretty much flat before you encounter another hill at the eighteenth so I managed the rest of the round okay until I reached the last hole. Once again I couldn't get up the hill on my own and it was a massive relief when I holed out to finish with a 74. There was no way I was able to play the second round the way I was feeling and I apologised to the tournament officials but said I simply couldn't carry on. I told them how bad I was feeling and they could obviously tell I was in a bit of a state. I had no choice but to pull out as there was no way I could have tackled those two hills a second time. I drove home resolving to see my doctor as soon as I could. When I thought back to the way I had felt at Quaker Ridge I realised there was obviously something wrong with me. I expected to be told I had some sort of virus. I certainly didn't expect the bombshell that was waiting just around the corner.

I went to see my doctor who didn't really seem to know what was wrong. He prescribed some painkillers and sent me away saying: 'It'll probably sort itself out.' This wasn't good enough. I had never had a day's illness in my life and I knew something was seriously wrong, so I went to see another doctor: my old friend Sarah Marr who, a few years earlier, had set me on the road to recovery from my chronic alcoholism. She was about to save my life for a second time.

Sarah realised right away that I was seriously ill and immediately sent me for an x-ray. She didn't tell me her suspicions then but I'm sure she already knew I had cancer. I went up to the Royal Alexandra Hospital in Paisley where they did the x-rays which clearly showed a shadow over my heart. I went back to Sarah to hear her verdict on the x-rays and said to her: 'I know it's bad so just give it to me straight.' So she did. She didn't mince her words at all. She just told me: 'Barclay, you've got leukaemia.' My whole world just caved in there and then. I didn't really know exactly what leukaemia was, but I knew it was cancer and I knew it was bad. In fact my first thought was: 'That's it, I'm dead.'

Even though I had known there was something wrong with me, I had tried to convince myself that it wasn't anything really serious. I thought it would turn out to be some sort of virus or infection; I would take a few pills and be as right as rain again a few weeks later. I suppose at the back of my mind there was the thought that it might be something more sinister, but I dismissed those thoughts telling myself: 'That sort of thing won't happen to me.' I certainly never believed for a second I could have cancer.

When Sarah delivered her bombshell there was no doubt in my mind that this was it; my life was all but over. Cancer was not something I knew much about and I just assumed I was going to die. But Sarah quickly made me realise that was not necessarily the case. She did not try to hide the pain and suffering that lay ahead, but she patiently explained the facts to me and gave me the belief that I could beat this dreadful illness. She said my chances of survival could be as high as 70 per cent and that helped give me the confidence I needed to fight it. However, as the next few months went by and I endured chemotherapy, radiotherapy, near-fatal infections and spent weeks on end barely able to lift my head off the pillow, there were times when that confidence and self-belief were put sorely to the test.

TISH HOWARD

Wife

Over the years I had become used to my father bringing
home fellow alcoholics he was trying to help. I had seen
plenty come and go, so I didn't think anything of it
when this stocky, mustachioed man walked through the
living-room door with dad. On that first night he stayed
until the early hours of the morning discussing his
problems with my father. In fact, after being introduced
to each other, Barclay and I hardly talked at all that
night. Over the next couple of weeks he came back to
the house regularly after Alcoholics Anonymous
meetings and we started talking more and more. He was
certainly a bit of a charmer and it wasn't long before he
was sending me flowers and asking me out. I can imagine
some women might not like the idea of going out with
somebody who had Barclay's problem, but it didn't
bother me at all. He told me what he was like when he
was drunk, how he would hurl abuse at anyone and
everyone, even his family and friends. He was
completely honest with me and told me how his
drinking had cost him his second marriage and led to
him losing an awful lot of friends. As I spoke to him,
though, I could barely believe he was the person he was
describing. He was such a gentleman – and also a gentle
man. He was kind, caring, compassionate and very easy-
going. It was impossible to picture him as the hard-
drinking, foul-mouthed lout that he was describing to
me. The fact that my father had gone through many of
the same experiences as Barclay also helped our

relationship. Some people who don't know much about alcoholism probably picture alcoholics as wasters who spend every waking moment drinking. Due to my dad's experiences, I knew that wasn't the case at all and Barclay's past didn't make me even hesitate about going out with him.

I had never been interested in golf before meeting Barclay, and even now don't really know very much about it. It's Barclay's thing and he just gets on with it, though I obviously take an interest in how he gets on if he is playing in a competition. Even with my lack of golfing knowledge, however, the 1997 Open was a time I will never forget. Laura-Jane and I went down to Troon for the last day and it was one of the most memorable days of my life. The atmosphere was absolutely brilliant, it was like nothing I had ever experienced before. While we were walking around the practice ground people were pointing and saying things like: 'There's Barclay Howard.' Laura-Jane could hear them and knew that her daddy was important that day, but had no idea why. She was only five at the time and thought it was terribly exciting that everyone knew her dad and that his picture was in all the newspapers. We both had a fantastic time on that Sunday. The roar of the crowd as Barclay made his way up the eighteenth was just unforgettable. I have never heard a noise like it. They were going wild, and when he holed out they probably gave him an even bigger cheer than Justin Leonard got when he sunk the winning putt. There was no way I could hold back the tears and I was crying with pride and happiness. I knew what Barclay had gone through and how low he had sunk, so it was hugely emotional for me to see him on top of the world. That's why it was so difficult to accept just a few weeks later that he had leukaemia and might die.

After Barclay got back from the Walker Cup in America we knew there was something wrong with him, but we had no idea it could be anything as serious as leukaemia. We thought he must have some sort of virus or was run-down from all the excitement and golf of the previous few weeks. When he told me he had cancer I was heartbroken.

The next year really was a living nightmare. I never drink alcohol, basically because I don't like the taste, but I very nearly turned to drink at that time. There were many nights I was at home crying my eyes out while Barclay was lying in hospital fighting for his life and I just thought, 'I'm going out to the shop to get a bottle.' The only thing that stopped me was knowing that even if I did get drunk the problem would still be there the next morning. I just didn't want to discuss it with anyone. I would go to the shops and well-meaning friends would ask how Barclay was getting on. But I was unable to discuss it without bursting into tears. It got to the stage where I would walk past people in the street I had known for years, completely ignoring them, in order to avoid speaking about Barclay. If I was at home I would just draw the curtains – even during the day – and refuse to answer the phone so that I could avoid having to see or speak to anyone. Sometimes I didn't even want to speak to my family because I found it easier to deal with the situation on my own. Instead there were a lot of times when I would phone Barclay's hospital ward in the early hours of the morning to talk to the nurses. I would beg them to tell me that Barclay was going to be all right, but of course there was no way they could do that. They would apologise and explain: 'We'd love to tell you he's going to be fine but we just can't promise that.'

Laura-Jane was only five and, although she knew her daddy was sick and in the hospital, she couldn't understand how serious it was. She would see me crying and beg me to stop. It was an incredibly difficult time for her, having one parent in hospital barely able to lift his head off the pillow, and another bursting into tears every time her daddy's name was mentioned. I really don't know how she coped. It was a real struggle for all of us especially as our hopes would keep getting raised then dashed. One day Barclay would seem to be doing well and I would be able to see some light at the end of the tunnel. Then the next day he'd suffer some sort of setback and I would feel we were back at square one again. One day we would be on cloud nine thinking he'd turned the corner, then the next we'd be at rock bottom again.

I really believe Laura-Jane was a huge factor in Barclay's recovery. He was so close to giving up at times that if it hadn't been for her then I think he would have just thrown in the towel. She is the most important thing in the world to him and he just showers her with affection. His love for her is undoubtedly what pulled him through.

Barclay has now come through two life-threatening illnesses and I am extremely proud of the way he has dealt with both of them. As I grew up seeing my father battle alcoholism I know how difficult it is to give up drinking. I know Barclay must feel like having a pint sometimes, but he manages to show great strength in resisting the temptation. He is a very determined man and that was demonstrated again when he was fighting leukaemia. Now he is over that he has another fight on his hands: the battle to get his strength back so he can play golf again at his former standard. I am desperate for him to do it because it was such a big part of his life and he really loves the game. He is working so hard on his strength and fitness that I know he is going in the right direction, but we both realise it is going to be a long battle. If there is one person, though, who can bounce back from all this, better and stronger than ever before, then it is my husband. He has set himself a goal of turning professional on the Senior Tour when he turns 50 in 2003 and I believe he will make it. Every day I pray to God that he does; because he's earned it.

NINE

'Please Kill Me'

The first thing that went through my mind once I had absorbed the shock of being told I could die from cancer was: 'What about my little girl?' Laura-Jane was only five at the time and as with all fathers and their young daughters she was the apple of my eye. All I could think was that I was not going to see my beautiful little girl grow up, that I wouldn't be there when she needed me. As I told the *Daily Telegraph*'s Robert Philip in an interview in April 1999: 'I didn't mind for myself – and I mean that, honestly – because, fair enough, I'd had a good run. But I want to see the wee one grow up, that's what worries me. It's such a bad, evil world out there, what with drugs and everything, that she'll need her dad. I have two teenage daughters from an earlier marriage who I never got to know because of the booze, so I'm not ready to die just yet when Laura-Jane's still so young.' This was something I was to keep in my mind throughout the long and difficult year I spent in hospital, unsure if I would live or die.

Inevitably I wondered if my illness was payback time for the way I had poisoned my body with booze for so long. Perhaps I even deserved this terrible disease. I asked one of my doctors if all the years of drinking had contributed to my cancer, but he assured me the type of leukaemia I had was probably unrelated. But I still wondered if I was being punished for the life I'd led for so long. It seemed so unfair that I could overcome that, and then be struck down with something as devastating as cancer. It was also hard to take in that one minute I could be playing great golf – the best of my life – then the next I had an illness that could kill me. When my doctor gave me the news it was like falling from the top of Everest to the bottom in a split second. Just six weeks earlier my life had seemed so perfect. Now here I was sitting in my doctor's office feeling like a dead man walking. I was shattered and thought that my days were numbered. It took a while for me to realise that, although I had an almighty fight on my hands, my life wasn't necessarily over. It just seemed like it at the time.

My treatment began on 12 September 1997 with a biopsy of the tumour that had been found in my chest. Apart from the cancer, I was also terrified about the treatment which lay ahead. I'd never had a day's illness in my life and now here I was with the disease everyone dreads above all others. The tumour was situated over my heart and this made it impossible for the doctors to cut it all out; so chemotherapy was needed to kill it and the infected blood cells before they could even think of giving me the stem cell transplant which was my only chance of living. When you have leukaemia your white blood cells become infected; eventually your immune system becomes useless and even the slightest infection would prove fatal. I needed the transplant to give me new, healthy cells which would then rebuild my immune system.

I had heard all the horror stories about chemotherapy, but not even they prepared me for the reality. It makes you so ill that at times you really would rather be dead. It also meant having to go into an isolation ward because I was so susceptible to infection.

I had to go through fortnightly doses of chemotherapy, but it was almost too much for me to endure. I was a big, 14 stone man and the treatment sapped every ounce of strength and spirit from me. In the hospital I came across young children who were undergoing the same treatment, yet brushing it aside like a minor inconvenience. To see a child so seriously ill, yet dealing with it with fortitude and strength of character made me feel ashamed at any trace of self pity.

At one stage, however, it really did become all too much and I truly wanted to end it all.

It was the only time I completely gave up. I had gone to Gartnavel Hospital, in the West End of Glasgow, for chemotherapy and it was a particularly bad dose. I felt awful and was in a tremendous amount of pain. My sister Morag came to visit me and was sitting by my bedside. I could barely move or speak, but I turned to her and asked her to help me die. I begged her: 'Will you just get me a jab to put me out of misery? I can't go on any more.' I was finished and really did just want the suffering to end. To see someone you love in such despair must be desperately difficult, especially when you know the only thing they want from you is the one thing you refuse to give them. Morag told the doctors what I had said and the specialist told me that if I ate for the next few days then I would be allowed home for a day. It was the motivation I needed. I had been at my lowest point, but suddenly I felt like I had won the Open. The thought of going home again, even for a day, quickly banished those dark thoughts and, I'm glad to say, I never sank that low again.

While Morag had, thankfully, refused the request I'd made of her, she was prepared to help me not long afterwards. Fortunately she was a lot more cooperative when it came to saving my life than she was when I wanted her to end it. In February 1998, she was the donor for the blood cell transplant which I prayed would cure me. It can be difficult finding the perfect match which is necessary for the transplant to succeed and blood relatives give the best hope – although it is still only a one-in-four chance. Luckily for me Morag's cells were a perfect match, but it was a tense time waiting for the transplant – in all probability the only chance I had of surviving – to go ahead.

The doctors told me that if it was a success it should send the cancer into remission for up to 30 years. But, even though I knew it was my only chance, I still dreaded the chemotherapy and radiation treatment which went with it. My discomfort wasn't helped by the fact that I can't stand the sight of needles. Not a good phobia to have when you seem to be getting an injection every five minutes.

The regular doses of chemotherapy could bring on diarrhoea, constipation, mouth ulcers and a tremendous amount of nausea. It was necessary to blast away all the remaining infected cells in my body, but I also needed a lumbar puncture so that the specialists could take a sample of my bone marrow. This involved inserting a needle into my spine before going into my hip for the sample. It's not an experience I would recommend if you have an option. Unfortunately I didn't.

A couple of entries in a diary I kept at this time aptly sum up the effect the chemotherapy had on me. On 31 January I wrote: 'Four hours of chemotherapy and I'm as sick as a dog. These are the worst symptoms I've suffered, but it was a heavy dose. At first if felt like the bad old days when I'd down five pints before going out for a game of golf. Now I'm nauseous all the time and can't look at anything to eat or drink.' The following day's entry reads: 'Flat on my back. The anti-sickness drugs help but I'm just waiting for the mouth ulcers to arrive. Still can't eat.' It also says: 'It would be easy to feel low, but the other patients are so positive. The staff are brilliant too.'

The chemotherapy went on for several months and left me completely shattered. It is administered through an intravenous drip and at the time seems to have no effect. In fact the first time I got it I wondered what all the fuss was about, but the next day felt like I was at death's door. Not every dose leaves you like that, fortunately, but most of them do. At one stage I had diarrhoea constantly for 16 weeks. There was nothing I could do about it and it would just come without warning. Several times a day the nurses would come and clean me up and change the sheets. At one stage they were even threatening to put a nappy on me and I had to beg them not to. I had little enough dignity left as it was, that really would have been the final straw! You really do start to wonder if it is worth going through with it all, then you think of the things that make it worthwhile. In my case it was my wife, daughter and the thought of playing the sport I loved so much again.

For the four days prior to the transplant I had to be taken twice a day from the Glasgow Royal to the Western Infirmary, a few miles away, for half-hour doses of radiotherapy. This was to kill all the remaining healthy blood cells in my body so that I was ready to accept Morag's. Again, this left me completely wiped out and barely able to speak. I had to just keep telling myself that, without it, I would die.

The lifesaving transplant took place on 5 February and took six hours to complete. For the next three weeks the doctors checked my blood eight times a day. I wrote on 24 February: 'So far so good. It's 19 days since the operation and things are going smoothly. The readings from the blood samples have been promising and Dr Ian Spence, my consultant, is confident. I feel like doing cartwheels. Even better – Morag has had no side effects. She's been brilliant.' However, just as I thought I had negotiated a safe passage through all the hazards, I found myself buried in deep, deep rough.

I was beginning to feel well again after the transplant and knew it wouldn't be long before I would be going home. I couldn't wait. One day I even felt up to walking to the hospital shop with Tish and my father-in-law, Davie, to buy an ice-cream. When we got back to my bed I was sitting up eating it when I suddenly collapsed. I knew nothing more until I woke up 36 hours later, feeling horrendous, and with a huge tube sticking out of my neck where they'd had to cut me open to allow me to breathe.

I had contracted a virus through an artificial vein which had been planted in my chest for the chemotherapy. My immune system had been unable to cope and for a few hours it was touch and go whether I was going to pull through. I also managed to crack my head on the floor as I fell and had to be wheeled through for a brain scan. Despite some reports, they did find one!

At least as I was unconscious I had no idea how seriously ill I was, but it must have been absolute hell for Tish. Once more she had to sit there completely helpless. She would have done anything to help me, but realistically all she could do was keep her fingers crossed and be there for me when I came round.

Worst of all, the blackout set my recovery back a long way. Before it, I was just two days away from being given the all-clear. Instead I was left feeling very sore, very ill and very, very low. I felt exhausted and could barely move. Even lifting a cup to my lips was too much effort and I began to despair about whether I would ever be able to swing a golf club again. In late March, however, I turned an important corner psychologically, though the circumstances surrounding it were tragic.

On 27 March another patient in my ward lost his fight, which left me feeling very distressed. He was in the bed directly across from me and I remember his wife and daughter visiting him. The pair of them started to scream wildly and I knew immediately what had happened. I felt so sorry for them, losing someone they loved so much to such a terrible illness. But it made me have a long, hard think and his death helped me realise that I couldn't give up. When you are as ill as I was it is hard to remain optimistic. There had been many moments when I felt so low that I wasn't sure I really wanted to carry on the fight. Strangely, this man's death gave me the will to continue fighting. I looked around the rest of the ward, saw what everyone else was going through and decided that if others were prepared to battle on to their last gasp then so was I. As I wrote in my diary at the time: 'I owe it to Tish and my wee girl.'

There is a lot of luck involved in fighting a disease like cancer. Treatment, the love of your family and your desire to beat it are all important, but at the end of the day some people, like me, are lucky and survive; others, like this poor husband and father whose loved ones were screaming across the ward from me, are not. I didn't deserve to live any more than him. He was just one of the unlucky ones. When you are trying to beat cancer, though, you have to be a bit selfish and while I really felt for his wife and daughter, I have to admit to feeling a sense of relief that it wasn't me lying dead with Tish and Laura-Jane crying at my bedside.

Each sufferer has to find their own way of dealing with the disease. Some want a string of visitors coming in from dawn to dusk, others, like me, prefer to be left in peace. I made a conscious decision to be something of a loner while I was ill. I didn't even watch television or listen to the radio, and the only time I read the papers was on a Monday to get the football and golf results. Tish came in to visit me daily, and Laura-Jane, my sister Morag, and my mother also visited regularly; but I was reluctant to see anyone else. Friends would often come to the hospital only to be told they couldn't see me. The last thing I wanted was for people to come in and tell me how well I was looking. It is a natural thing for friends to do, but I knew they would just be saying it to make me feel better and it wouldn't have worked. I could see in the mirror how bad I looked. I hope they realise I wasn't being rude, I was just dealing with my illness in my own way. As I said, you have to be a bit selfish and that means putting your own wishes first. I hope no one was offended when I wouldn't see them and understand that it was just my way of dealing with my situation. One person I was glad to see, however, was my friend Gary Lewis, a chef who would make up wonderful meals and bring them to the hospital to keep my strength up.

Even at the beginning of April, I was still barely able to lift my head from the pillow and I seemed to be sleeping day and night. The doctors said they wouldn't let me go home until I started eating properly and put on some weight. I was still feeling so ill that I couldn't stand the thought of food, so for six weeks I was fed through a tube in my nose. It was thoroughly unpleasant, but it was the start I needed and once the tube came out I felt ready to tackle food again. On 15 April I actually managed to lift back my bed covers – and got the fright of my life. I hadn't been prepared for the extent of muscle wastage I had suffered. Ninety per cent of my muscles had vanished; I mean, my thighs looked more like ankles. I really did look like I had just got out of a prisoner of war camp. But, determined to prove to the doctors, and more importantly myself, that I was on the mend, I somehow swung my legs over the side of the bed, stood up and started to walk. I only managed two steps before slumping back on to the bed completely exhausted, but it was a start. By the end of the month I was able to take a dozen steps at a time and was getting some physiotherapy to help build up my muscles again.

On 9 May, I got the news I seemed to have been waiting an eternity to hear. Dr Spence, who ran the haematology unit at Glasgow Royal Infirmary, told me the transplant had been a success, my blood count was clear and I was going to make it. My diary adequately records my feelings for that day. 'After seven months of hell, here is the light at the end of the tunnel. I can feel tears well up. Straight away I rung Tish and we had a wee bubble together.' Then, to top everything, I was told that I could go home the next day.

It was the day I had feared I would never see. During my darkest hours in hospital the only thing that had kept me going was a picture in my mind of being back at home, laughing and joking with Tish and Laura-Jane. It was a wonderful feeling as Tish helped me to pack my belongings and I said goodbye to the doctors and nurses who had done so much for me. It was also fairly emotional saying goodbye to the other patients. I prayed that every one of them would also be going home soon; in reality I knew many of them would not. It was very humbling to be surrounded by other patients in the cancer ward and realise that no matter how ill or close to death I had been, I was still the lucky one. It's a terrible cliché, I know, but at times like that you become acutely aware how true it is that there is always someone worse off than yourself. I saw a lot of people pass away while I was in hospital. This included young people, which I found incredibly hard to cope with. There was one occasion, after I left hospital, when a nurse rang me at home to say that a young Celtic fan I had become friendly with was refusing to eat. She wanted me to go up to the hospital and see if I could cheer him up. We arranged a time and, a few hours later, I was just about to leave when the phone rang again. The nurse told me that the boy had said he didn't want to see anyone that day but could I come tomorrow? Of course I agreed, but, tragically, the lad died that night. If ever I needed any further proof of what a terrible, terrible illness cancer is, that was it.

I felt almost guilty as I headed home, knowing that I did not deserve to survive any more than any of the other poor souls in that ward. I knew that some of the friends I had made in there and was leaving behind would not be as lucky. There were difficult times where you would look across the ward and see an empty bed where someone you'd become good friends with had been lying the night before. No matter how positive you are, things like that make you wonder if you're going to be next. I had also seen other patients who had arrived at the same time as me get better and go home which, while I was pleased for them, had left me feeling pangs of jealousy. As I left I wished everyone else the best, and I really did hope each of them would be cured, but realistically I knew that would never happen. In later months when I would go back to hospital for check-ups I would ask about some of the patients I'd known in my ward. The first five I asked about had all died. I stopped asking about anyone else after that as the answers were too painful to deal with. I was so grateful to be on my way home. But I realised I had an obligation to every one of the patients in there who didn't go home, to make the most of the rest of my life. That included a determination to get back to golf and not just to enjoy the odd round on a Sunday afternoon, but to play competitively again at the standard I had reached in 1997 – or better. If I thought the future was going to be all rosy, however, I was badly mistaken.

When I got home I was so weak that my father-in-law Davie and brother-in-law Robert had to carry me into the house. I couldn't even drive myself there because I wasn't strong enough to press the accelerator. When I wanted to go out I had to slide down the steps from our first floor flat on my backside before Tish helped me into a borrowed wheelchair at the bottom. It was all pretty undignified to say the least, but I didn't care. I was just happy to be home with my family and finally on the mend – or so I thought.

I had been home for just two days when I started to feel unwell. I woke up in the night feeling freezing cold, but sweating so much my eyes were stinging. When Tish touched me she said I was burning up. She had no choice but to call an ambulance. The paramedics knew immediately I was seriously ill and decided they didn't have time to take me even the handful of miles from my home in Johnstone to the specialist unit at Glasgow Royal Infirmary. Instead they took me to the nearer Royal Alexandra Hospital in Paisley. In the ambulance I was screaming from the incredible pain I was feeling in my knee joints. I had never known anything like it. It was absolute agony. When we got to the hospital I begged the nurses to give me diamorphine for the pain. Once again, I thought I was dying. The doctors diagnosed septicaemia and later told me that when I arrived I was only 20 minutes from dying. Septicaemia is blood poisoning and it left me in agony. I honestly thought that my time was up. After all I had been through, and just as it looked like I was going to pull through, I couldn't believe something else was being thrown at me. Fortunately, thanks to the wonderful care of the doctors and nurses at the Royal Alexandra and Glasgow Royal, where I was transferred to, I recovered and a month later was once again able to go home to my family. But

I knew there was still a long way to go before I would be anywhere near back to full health.

No matter how much encouragement and goodwill you receive from those you love, as well as complete strangers, it is still difficult not to lose hope on occasion when you're involved in the kind of long and painful fight I was going through. In May 1998, while I was in hospital recovering from the septicaemia, I was at one of my lowest points emotionally and genuinely believed I wouldn't make it. This wasn't like the time I asked Morag to help me die; I just couldn't see how I was ever going to get better. My arms were positively skeletal because of the massive amount of muscle wastage and even talking to my wife and daughter was a huge effort. I was so certain I was going to die that I asked Tish to contact my lawyer Ian Briggs so I could make a will. I wasn't being morbid or giving up, I was just being practical. Ian had been a friend for a long time and agreed I was doing the right thing. So he drew up the will, I signed it and it was witnessed by one of the nurses in the ward. I have to say it wasn't terribly difficult deciding who would get what. These things are easy when you're poor! I think there will be a lot more interest in who I'm leaving my golf clubs to than my not very considerable fortune. Fortunately the will has not been needed yet, so the details of who will get my favourite putter will have to remain secret for a little while longer yet.

After recovering from the septicaemia I got out of hospital again in June but was quickly back in, this time suffering from dehydration. I had also lost even more weight and at one stage was weighing less than nine stone. I stayed in hospital this time until September 1998, a year after I had first gone into hospital. Since then I've had the odd brief spell back in when there has been a minor setback in my recovery, such as migraines and a bout of shingles, but nothing too serious, thank goodness. Now it was a case of building up my strength and putting some weight back on so I could start cracking balls up the fairway again.

When you are trying to beat something like cancer it's important to set yourself goals or targets, I quickly discovered. Sometimes promising yourself even a small treat can be a tremendous spur. So you can imagine how motivating it was for me to receive an invitation from the R&A to go to watch my pals from the Great Britain and Ireland side taking on the Americans in the Walker Cup at the wonderful Highland course of Nairn in September 1999. I was determined to be well enough and, when I arrived, I gritted my teeth and told the journalists taking a great interest in my visit: 'I'm staying here as long as it takes for us to win.' When I was asked how I was feeling after the journey I tried to inject a bit of humour by saying: 'I'm still breathing and that's the main thing.' But I think that quote made some of them worry that I could drop dead at any minute!

I arrived the day before the competition started and it was very emotional to read in the papers the next day what some of the players had said about me. Gary Wolstenholme was quoted as saying: 'Just having Barclay here has been inspirational. The players really appreciate him making the effort. When I stood on the twelfth tee in practice today and I wasn't hitting the ball well, I suddenly thought that was *nothing* in comparison to what Barclay's been through. I used to call Barclay my little tank engine because you just wind him up and send him off. He's lost a lot of weight but the character is still inside him. It's great to see him.' Very kind words which brought a lump to my throat when I read them.

I spent the competition going round the course with team captain Peter McAvoy in his buggy, urging the boys on. It was a brilliant experience and was even more nerve-racking than playing. The R&A also looked after me superbly all weekend and they put me up in the same hotel as the players. I was really made to feel like one of the team. I was invited to an official dinner one night with about 350 guests and I was sitting across the table from the wonderful commentator Peter Allis. During the speeches, an official from the R&A said how great it was to see Barclay Howard and the whole place got to its feet and gave me a three minute standing ovation. I wanted to get up as well but Peter Allis told me just to stay where I was. It took every ounce of strength I had not to burst into tears at this wonderful gesture. That night and the weekend in general gave me a huge lift. Then when we defeated the Yanks, that added the icing on the cake.

As I said earlier, all sorts of things can give you a lift and raise your spirits when you're enduring one of the many black periods you go through while fighting cancer. Watching some of my closest friends thrash the Americans at Nairn was a definite highlight of 1999. But it wasn't the only one.

My close friend Dean Robertson, by this time playing on the European Tour, also gave me a huge spur when he won his first title as a professional. He called me up from Rome where he had just lifted the Italian Open and told me: 'Barclay, this is dedicated to you.' When he was interviewed later Dean said: 'The news seemed to lift his voice.' If only he knew how much! In some ways I think his win gave me more pleasure than it did him.

Another close friend, Graham Rankin, also had kind words to say after he won the Scottish Amateur Championship in 1998. Graham would call me regularly to see how I was, offer words of encouragement and generally cheer me up. But he didn't get in touch at all during the Scottish Amateur. It was only afterwards that he revealed why. As soon as he had sunk the winning putt he told reporters: 'I haven't spoken to Barclay this week as I wanted to remain focused, but when the presentation's over I'll be on the phone. He's doing a bit better every day and hopefully news of my win will pick him up a little.' I later joked with Graham that he should enjoy every minute of his year as Scottish Amateur champion, because I would be back in 1999 to regain the title I'd won three years earlier. Sadly, I still wasn't strong enough to play in 1999 and Graham has since turned professional and is now doing well on the European Tour. But I plan to be back in the game soon, showing the rest of the guys I can still play a bit.

I also received hundreds of cards from well-wishers all over the world and every one helped a little bit. Many were from people I had never even met before, they just remembered the Open at Troon then heard what had happened to me afterwards. One card, from French international Laurent Bailly, said: 'I just wanted, on behalf of all the French team, to wish you a recovery as quick as possible. There are still a lot of good fights to happen between our two countries and it is a must that you take part in them.' Downing Gray, who captained the US team in my two Walker Cup matches wrote: 'Word has reached me regarding your current physical skirmish. Your many friends on this side of the Atlantic hope for a speedy recovery. You are in our prayers and I am certain your will-power will serve you well now, as it has in the past, both on and off the golf course.' Bob Torrance dropped me a line on the eve of my operation to say: 'If it's the Barclay I know then you'll come through with flying colours.' A woman in Aberdeen wrote to me after reading about my illness in her local newspaper. Her letter said: 'My husband and I were at the Open in Troon every day and took great pleasure in watching you play. I'm not ashamed to say I had tears in my eyes watching you walk up the eighteenth on the final day. So you hang in there and rest assured there's lots of people thinking of you and your family at this time.' One fellow amateur competitor, Dougie McKinnon, cheekily wrote that when he heard of my illness he immediately entered a string of competitions 'while there is a chance of winning something!' I also got cards from various tournaments which had been signed by all the competitors and officials. I even got a phone call while I was in hospital from the president of the Pine Valley Golf Club in America – one of the most famous courses in the world. He told me he was in his 70s and had beaten cancer and was back playing golf again. He told me that he knew I could do the same and we had a long chat about what he had gone through and what I was facing. For somebody in his position to take the time to track me down like that and give me a call was a great source of inspiration.

Bob Champion, the jockey who overcame cancer to win the 1981 Grand National on Aldaniti, also had hugely encouraging words of support. His advice was: 'Just think about coming back and winning the Open.' He also said in a newspaper interview: 'Barclay proved he was a fighter in the Open – and he's got to be a fighter now. He must set ambitious goals and go for them. In my case the initial feeling was one of devastation, but you can't afford to let that feeling linger. I just said to myself "I am not going to die" and made plans to beat the disease. I'm not saying it was my attitude that cured me – but it helped.' His words were spot on. Bob also said he believed that if you are a fierce competitor in sport, it applies in life as well. He added that throughout his treatment he kept thinking about riding to victory in the Grand National. I may not win the Open, but just dreaming about it while I was lying in my hospital bed, racked with pain and dreading my next dose of chemotherapy, certainly helped. Bob's words were a definite inspiration to me. All these little messages of support gave me small lifts.

Despite all these morale-boosting moments, there were others which left me sad and deflated. One was the 1998 Open at Royal Birkdale. Twelve months earlier at Troon I had gained worldwide fame as I enjoyed the greatest moment of my life, winning the Silver Medal for best amateur. Now I was at home, weak and tired, with the idea of swinging a golf club ever again seeming little more than a fanciful dream. I kept telling everyone I would be back playing soon, but I'm sure some people didn't believe me, no matter how much they wanted to.

The biggest problem, once I had got home to continue my recovery, was boredom. I was used to working and playing golf every day and now all I could do was sit around and watch television. There is only so much excitement you can gain from taking 30 tablets a day. Fortunately my employers, the golf club manufacturers John Letters, were extremely understanding about my illness and allowed me all the time off that I needed. They had also made me a new set of clubs which I was itching to try out, but they just had to sit in my hallway for months. Any golfer will understand how frustrating that was, but knowing they were there waiting for me was another motivation. The staff at the factory in the Hillington area of Glasgow also had a whip round for me while I was in hospital so I could go away for a weekend with Tish and Laura-Jane. Again, a lovely and hugely appreciated gesture.

The closer the 1998 Open came, the more I wished I could have been there. It was a strange experience watching it on the television with Tish and Laura-Jane, remembering how happy I had been just 12 months earlier and how proud they were of me; then thinking about the traumas we had all shared since then. Once again, however, I realised there was no point in feeling sorry for myself and tried to use the experience in a positive way, telling myself I would be back at the Open. Any time I've needed motivation I've thought of that goal and still think of it. It's not just a dream, I *know* I'm going to be playing there again.

Throughout my year of hospitals, traumas and near-death experiences there were two constants in my life: my wife Tish and daughter Laura-Jane. To watch somebody you love in great pain and quite possibly dying is a dreadful experience. No wife should have to go through the agonies of knowing her husband would rather be dead than alive. Yet Tish was an absolute rock all the way through. In all the time I was in hospital there was only one day when she didn't visit, when she had a bug. She would arrive around noon and stay until she had to leave at night. Most afternoons she would just fall asleep beside me and the nurses would bring her a blanket to make sure she was warm enough. Then we would wake up and chat some more and she'd tell me how Laura-Jane was getting on as well as all the other family news and gossip from around Johnstone. She also knew I couldn't stand the hospital food and would make meals at home to bring with her. In many ways it was every bit as gruelling a time for her as it was for me. Apart from her daily visits to the hospital, she had to run a household and, for a year, bring up Laura-Jane without me. On top of all that she knew she could never let herself seem down when she visited me, no matter how bad she felt. She knew how important it was that she remained positive and strong throughout and without that I would never have made it.

Tish has now saved my life twice. If I hadn't met her I have little doubt that I would have drunk myself to death by now. I had lost a lot of friends because of my drinking, but she stuck by me and, when I felt myself wavering and desperate for a drink, gave me the strength to battle on. There is also no way I would have got out of the cancer ward alive without her love and support. She and Laura-Jane gave me the desire to get better. All that time I knew I had to get well for them. I just couldn't bear the thought of leaving them behind to struggle on without me. Without that motivation there's no way I would have pulled through.

For a five-year-old, as Laura-Jane was at the time, seeing your daddy as ill as I was must be a terrifying and immensely confusing experience. Tish and I told her that I was ill and that my hair was going to fall out, but we never told her I might die. How on earth do you explain that to a young child? But despite our best efforts to let her know what was happening she still had no idea what was going on. My weight dropped from 14 stone to 10 in about six weeks; my hair fell out and I could walk no more than a few yards. Seeing her daddy like that had a tremendous impact on Laura-Jane's life – as it must with every other child who has a seriously ill parent. I did not want her to come to the hospital too often because it was not the sort of place where a young child should have to spend too much time. But when she did visit it was a huge inspiration. Every time I set eyes on her as she came into the ward it strengthened my resolve to get better. She would always do her best to be cheerful even though she was obviously very distressed at seeing me so ill, and it hurt like hell spending a year watching her grow up but unable to do anything for her. Eventually the strain of it all took its toll on Laura-Jane as she became increasingly upset and confused at what was happening to me. In the end she had to go to a child psychiatrist for counselling which was an immense help and she's now doing very well at school. She has even taken up golf and seems to be very keen. I'm not sure if Tish is pleased about this or not! Having no interest in the sport whatsoever, she's probably just dreading all the boring golf talk over the dinner table.

My remarkable sister Morag also deserves praise. She saw me at my lowest point, when I begged her to help me die, yet has been there whenever I've needed her. She gave me the blood cells which saved my life and was prepared to donate her bone marrow, an extremely painful procedure, if I'd needed it. Fortunately I didn't.

For my mother, Wilhelmina, it was a traumatic time. No parent ever expects to see their child die and it must have been awful for her to see me so close to death, especially after the way I had overcome the earlier problems in my life.

These are the four women in my life and I love them all dearly for what they have been through with me. Ladies, I couldn't have made it without you.

The doctors and nurses at the various hospital units where I have spent so much time also deserve an enormous amount of praise and thanks. Every single one of them is an inspiration and you want to get well as a way of thanking them for all the effort they put in on your behalf. Cancer is such a dreadful illness and has such a devastating effect on those unlucky enough to suffer from it that it must be hard for such caring people to deal with it on a daily basis. Yet their dedication, professionalism and optimism never waver. They are a truly remarkable set of people.

MORAG NICHOL

Sister

To see someone you love lying in a hospital bed in immense pain, begging you to help them die, is an experience no one should have to go through. To see

Barclay, my only brother, in agony and watch him completely lose the will to live was absolutely heartbreaking. I am sure that a lot of people who are seriously ill sometimes think it would be easier just to end it all. And there is no doubt that Barclay meant every word when he said he couldn't stand the pain and sickness any more and begged me to end his life. I just stared at him, both of us with tears in our eyes, and for a few seconds I was lost for words. Then I realised this was Barclay at his lowest and the only way to go was up. It was the day I had gone to the hospital to be tested to see if my cells were a match for Barclay's so the transplant could go ahead. The doctors were having real trouble taking blood from him because of the state his body was in by this stage. We knew that a transplant from me was the best chance Barclay had of surviving, so we were terrified that our cells would not be a match, but still I couldn't believe he had sunk so low. It was tragic seeing and hearing him in that state. But I knew I had to be strong. The only way he was going to come through this illness was with the strength and support of those closest to him. So I just said: 'Barclay, don't be so stupid. This is going to work and you have to be positive.' I told him that I didn't believe he really wanted to die and just kept trying to reassure him that he would get through it. I told him he had to think about people other than just himself. 'Think of the people you love and who love you that you'll be leaving behind if you die.' I told him again and again. I made him think about his little girl Laura-Jane and I believe she was the single most important person in his recovery. I don't think he could bear the thought of dying and leaving her behind. He knew how much she needed her daddy and it was for her more than anything else that he decided to carry on fighting.

I am sure that a lot of seriously ill people go through those low points where they don't think they can go on any further. Hopefully, however, they will be able to draw some strength and hope from Barclay. There is no doubt that he really wanted to die. He did. He'd had enough. Luckily, though, he came to his senses and bravely fought on, through all the pain, the sickness and the seemingly endless days lying in bed barely able to move. Eventually, he beat the cancer and was once again able to be the wonderful husband and father he had been before. It was a long, long battle and at times I did wonder whether he would make it. Like everyone else, I had to just keep hoping and praying.

When I heard he had leukaemia I could hardly believe my ears. Barclay had never been ill in his life; in fact nobody in the family had been. We even tried to remember if any one of us had been really sick and the best we could come up with was a dose of measles or chickenpox as kids. So to be told that Barclay was suffering from something as serious as leukaemia was a tremendous shock. I first learned about his illness when his wife Tish phoned to tell me and ask if I would tell our mother as she thought she would find it easier to hear the news from me. When I went to tell mum I don't think she really realised how serious it was, but after a couple of days, when she'd had time to think about it, she knew Barclay was in a very bad way. It must have been very hard for her to visit him in hospital and see how poorly he was. Now, when I think back to what he went through during all that time in hospital, I'm incredibly proud of my brother. He suffered in a way that nobody should have to, but he came through.

Watching him fight leukaemia was a very different experience from watching his battle with alcoholism. I had always known that Barclay liked a drink, of course, but it took me a long time to realise he had a problem. Not as long as it took him, admittedly, but it wasn't until about 1987 that I began to realise my brother was an alcoholic. After it became obvious that he had a serious problem I did what any sister would do and sat him down to try to talk to him about it. As with an awful lot of people with his condition, however, he just wouldn't accept that he had a problem. Obviously it didn't occur to him that it wasn't normal behaviour for a golfer to pack his bag with cans of lager to drink on the way round so that he wouldn't get the shakes while putting!

He really needed a shock to make him see sense. My husband, Bob, and I tried again and again but he just wouldn't listen. Part of the difficulty was that he had been so good at hiding the problem that for a long time we didn't know how bad things had got. We only really got to the bottom of it properly a short time before his ban from golf. It didn't matter what we said, Barclay would tell us he was fine and we were worrying about nothing. He would eventually admit he had a bit of a problem, but would assure us that he could handle it. Obviously he was trying to convince himself as much as us. The only difference was that he believed what he was saying.

The ban from Cochrane Castle was definitely the incident which turned his life around. He had loved golf since he was a small boy and to be told that he was not allowed to play hit him really, really hard. At that point there were two things that could have happened: he could either have gone off the rails completely, or he could admit to himself he had a drink problem and do something about it. I'm glad to say he chose the second option. But, even though he knew it was for his own good, the next few months were very hard for Barclay. I am so proud of the way he has turned his life round. The Open at Troon in 1997 was the crowning moment and I'll never forget how proud the whole family were of him that week. For him to fall ill the way he did was so unfair. Just when he seemed to have put all the bad times behind him and he'd settled down with his lovely wife and daughter and was playing the best golf of his life, he was struck down with cancer. That was a cruel blow, but now he's better and, with Tish and Laura-Jane's help, putting his life back together again. There are now only three things Barclay needs in his life to make him happy: his wife, his daughter and his golf. I'm just so pleased he's still able to enjoy them all.

TEN

Back on the Tee

Throughout the long, painful months I had spent in hospital and recuperating at home I had dreamed of playing golf again. At times it seemed a somewhat fanciful notion which stood no chance of being realised. As I lay in bed racked with pain and barely able to open my eyes, as I felt so ill from the effects of the chemotherapy, I wondered how I was even going to live, far less play golf. But through it all I kept telling myself I would be back out there again some day. Not only that, I swore I would come back better than ever. After all, I had done it once before after my ban in 1991. I barely lifted a club for a year then found the motivation to work harder at my game than ever before; with the result that I started producing the best golf of my life. If I could do it once then I could do it again, I figured. This time round, however, it wasn't to be quite that simple.

It was March 2000 before I was finally able to hit a golf ball again; two and a half years since that day at the Largs-Kelburne course where I'd almost collapsed walking up the hill at the first hole. I had been desperate to give it a go earlier, but I knew rushing things would not do me any good. Finally, I felt strong enough to hit a few shots. I didn't want an audience of people I knew gawping at me so, instead of going to Cochrane Castle, I headed for a driving range in Johnstone run by a friend, Ronnie Docherty. As I stood in my bay, addressing the ball and looking out over the range I remembered exactly how much golf meant to me. It seemed incredible that I could have gone so long without hitting a ball. As soon as I started my backswing it felt like the most natural thing in the world to me. You know how sometimes when you meet up with an old friend you've not seen for a long time and you just pick up exactly where you left off without any feelings of awkwardness? Well, that's how the first shot that day felt. Obviously I was rusty and, because I was about four stone lighter than the last time I'd played and still very weak, I couldn't hit the ball nearly as well as I used to. But that didn't matter. I was hitting it and that was all that counted. Even if it only went 50 yards, I just loved the feeling of swinging a club and making contact with a ball again. It was like returning home after being away at sea for several years. That first day I really only hit a handful of shots and was absolutely exhausted afterwards. It was ironic to think that I used to hit hundreds of shots every day and now I was worn out after a few gentle chips. I didn't care how tired I was, though. It was a start and I was determined to build on it.

I continued to go to the driving range most days and gradually built up my strength and energy. While I was still hugely underweight and far from completely healthy, I felt I was making progress. In fact, after a couple of months I felt I had completely regained my touch. My pitching and putting felt as good as they had ever done. The only problem was that my lack of strength and weight meant I couldn't get any distance on the ball. In spite of this I reckoned I was in good enough shape to return to tournament golf and in June entered the Jimmy Heggarty Trophy, a 36-hole tournament played at the Cathkin Braes course which I had won a couple of times before. I knew I had no chance of winning. In fact I knew there was every chance I would come last. I didn't care. I just wanted to feel the buzz again that went with playing in a tournament. I didn't care if I took all day to get round and shot hundreds, I'd set myself the target of playing and I was determined to achieve it.

I knew I wouldn't be able to lug my clubs round the course, even on a trolley, so I got myself a caddie for the day – Tish. It would be safe to say she wasn't the best caddie in the world, not knowing the difference between a putter and a driver obviously proved a hindrance, but there was no way she was going to let me go out there without her. She was determined to keep as close an eye on me as she could and reckoned that caddying would be the best way to do that. I explained to the tournament organisers that it would be impossible for me to play both the rounds and said that if it was a problem for them I would fully understand and not play, but they welcomed me with open arms. In fact, the reception they gave me was tremendous and they told me they would be happy for me to play as many or as few holes as I liked. They said they were just delighted to see me out there playing again. It was exactly the sort of response I'd hoped for.

I was drawn to play with the Cathkin Braes club champion, Ian Mackie, who I knew from past tournaments. He is an extremely warm character and he could not have been any kinder to me that day – although he probably thought I could have picked a better caddie! As I said at the start of this book, standing on the first tee was a nerve-racking experience. I thought of everything I had been through and couldn't believe

I was actually back playing tournament golf again. It was a prospect that had seemed impossible at times over the previous two and a half years; but here I was, with my driver in my hands, addressing the ball and about to hit my first competitive shot for a long time. If it had been a Hollywood movie I'm sure I would have sent the ball soaring 300 yards straight up the middle of the fairway. Sadly, though, this was reality and what happened next was almost the most embarrassing moment of my career.

As I knew I was lacking strength and power I decided to give it everything I had to try and get a bit of distance on the ball. I basically tried to smack the ball into the middle of next week – just about the most basic golf error there is. The first thing beginners are told is not to try to hit the ball too hard because you will never hit it cleanly. Well, I certainly proved that to be correct as I topped my drive for the first time in more than 30 years. I smacked the ball straight into the ground about two inches in front of where I'd teed it up, then watched in horror as it trundled about 40 yards up the fairway. I was mortified and just wanted the ground to eat me up. I immediately apologised to Ian and anyone else who was around. I thought about blaming my caddie but even Tish realised what a hash I had made of my drive so I didn't think I'd much chance of getting away with that ploy! I ended up taking a triple bogey seven at the hole, but at least I was back in tournament golf. I kept apologising to Ian for walking so slowly and taking so many shots but he couldn't have been more understanding and enouraged me all the way round. At one stage I offered to just pack up and go if he felt I was putting him off in any way, but he told me that we would go round together and even if I needed to stop for a rest then that would be fine with him. He said he would stick with me all the way round no matter how long it took.

The funny thing was that my short game was in great shape. My chipping was working really well and once I got on to the greens I just seemed to be holing everything. My putting was on fire. The only problem was the number of shots it was taking me to get to the greens! I was so weak that I just couldn't get any distance on the ball at all. By the time we had finished, and I'd shot 83, I was absolutely exhausted. Not just because of how far I had walked, but also because I'd had to hit so many woods on the way round as it was the only way I could get the ball to go more than about 100 yards.

Afterwards I collapsed into my seat in the clubhouse and thought about my round. I couldn't remember the last time I had taken 83 shots in a round of golf, yet I couldn't remember the last time I had felt as much satisfaction. It was the worst score I had recorded for years and I was still as happy as a pig in mud. I had played a full round of golf for the first time in two and a half years and it wouldn't have bothered me if I had taken 183. The only downside was that I felt like I needed to sleep for about a week, and my trusty caddie wasn't in much better shape! I said to the tournament referee: 'I'm really sorry but there's no way I can go out again for the second round.' He just looked at me and said: 'That's fine Barclay. We are just so pleased to see you playing again.' And I was just so pleased to be playing again. Since the day I first picked up a golf club I had loved the game and to be too ill to play for such long time had caused me as much pain as my illness. I have always relished the challenge of trying to get better at golf and attempting to beat my best scores. It was almost like an addiction for me.

While my score in the Jimmy Heggarty Trophy that day was one of my worst ever in a competitive event I still remember it as one of the best days of my life. It was just so enjoyable to be out there again on a golf course competing, even if it was really just with myself. I had completed a round of golf and that meant I had won my own personal competition that day. I just assumed that I would get stronger and better as the months went by. Sadly, this wasn't to be the case. I played two more events that summer and in both could only manage one round, shooting in the mid-'80s each time. My strength just wasn't coming back and I started to get depressed. My close friend Dean Robertson, the European Tour player who I used to play with at Cochrane Castle, reminded me that I had to take things one day at a time. I thought that once I'd beaten the leukaemia then everything else would just fall into place quickly. The doctors had warned me not to expect too much too soon but I was very impatient. It took Dean to remind me that I shouldn't expect miracles. He made me realise that I was lucky just to be alive and that anything else is a bonus. Of course he was right, but it is hard to see things that way when you feel so desperate for everything to return to normal.

I now realise of course that sending the cancer into remission was only the start of the recovery process from leukaemia, not the end. I had originally expected to be back to full health and playing golf like the old days by the time the 2001 season came round, but when it did I was still a long way from full fitness. No matter what I ate I struggled to put on any weight. I was also doing weight training every day and practising my swing with a specially-made club filled with lead, which weighed five pounds. I was also going to the driving range every day, often at five o'clock in the morning, and was hitting the ball as well as ever. However, I still had the same problem of lacking strength which meant lack of distance.

That summer I was also affected by a very bad stiffening in my muscles, a reaction to the stem cells transplanted from Morag. This was treated with a course of steroids but it still remains to be seen how long it will take to shake off. The doctors have told me that, even though the leukaemia may be beaten, it can take several years to fully recover my health; so I am trying to be patient and can see gradual improvements which spur me on.

I missed out on my chance of turning professional when I was a young man, but the burgeoning success of the Senior Tour means I will have a second chance to earn a living playing the game I love. I will qualify for the Seniors when I turn 50 in 2003 and my next major target is to turn professional then. I am extremely lucky to be surrounded by so many people who love and encourage me – especially Tish. She has been the most wonderful wife over the years. There is no question that if I hadn't had her and Laura-Jane I would have just given up during my long fight with cancer. Their love was my inspiration to get better. Now Tish is as eager as I am for me to get back to playing top-quality golf again, and Dean Robertson has generously offered to sponsor me when I hit the Seniors Tour. He is one of a number of friends whose support has been invaluable over the years and I am eternally grateful to every one of them.

Now all I can do is follow my doctor's orders carefully and keep my fingers crossed that I will return to full health as soon as possible. I said earlier that there is a lot of luck involved in beating cancer and the same is true of the recovery afterwards. Some people return to normal very quickly while others can take years to recover. While I am seeing small improvements in my health, I know it is taking a long time. I also know, though, that I could wake up one morning and feel much better. When that happens I will be ready to take full advantage.

As Dean said, all I can do is take it one day at a time and hope for the best; so that's what I'm doing. I know that sooner or later I will be back to full fitness, and when I am I know my golf will be better than ever. When you have been as close to death as I have, the thought of standing over a crucial six foot putt doesn't hold quite the same sort of fears. That's why I know I will be a success on the Seniors Tour when I turn professional more than 30 years after I should have done.

However, it is the Open that most people remember me for, so I am desperate to have another go at that – either as an amateur or professional. Funnily enough the 2004 championship is being held at a course I've fond memories of – Royal Troon.